T0355943

Isaac Bashevis Singer

Writings on Yiddish and Yiddishkayt
A Spiritual Reappraisal, 1946-1955

Isaac Bashevis Singer

Writings on Yiddish and Yiddishkayt
A Spiritual Reappraisal, 1946–1955

TRANSLATED AND EDITED BY DAVID STROMBERG

Isaac Bashevis Singer: Writings on Yiddish and Yiddishkayt, Vol. II: A Spiritual Reappraisal, 1946–1955
Translated and edited by David Stromberg

White Goat Press, the Yiddish Book Center's imprint
Yiddish Book Center
Amherst, MA 01002
whitegoatpress.org

Printed in the United States of America at The Studley Press, Dalton, MA
10 9 8 7 6 5 4 3 2 1

Paperback ISBN 979-8-9894524-7-7
Hardcover ISBN 979-8-9894524-8-4
Ebook ISBN 979-8-9894524-9-1

Library of Congress Control Number: 2024940440

Book and cover design by Michael Grinley

*This book has been made possible with
generous support from Robert L. Friedman*

To the victims and survivors of October 7, 2023
—David Stromberg

Table of Contents

Introduction: A Testament to the Spirit 13

The Eternal Jewish Question: What's the Purpose?. . . 25

On the Question of Style in Yiddish Literature 31

They Were in the Nazi Hell and Still Did Not
Lose Their Faith in Humanity 39

The Philosophy of Our Prophets 45

Jewish Tragedy Should Not Be Made Mundane 53

Our Language, Our Literature 59

Modern Jews and Their Internal Conflict 69

On the Revival of Yiddish Culture in America 75

A New Yiddish Literary Group? 81

The Nature of Our Literature through the Ages 89

The Synagogue and the Studyhouse 97

Old Religious Books Reprinted in America 103

What Is the Foundation of Jewish Culture? 109

Righteous and Wicked—Words We No
Longer Use 117

Jews and the Rule of Law 123

Americanism and Jewishness 131

Philosophers and the *U'Netaneh Tokef* Prayer 139

Everyday Jews—Yesterday and Today 145

Yiddish Literature Does Not Portray the
Great Events of Our Time 153

Jews and the World 163

Small Shtetl, Big Swamp 173

The Concept of Beauty among Olden Jews 183

In My Father's Courtroom 191

When Actions Achieve Nothing 199

Is There a Way Out for Yiddish Literature? 205

Acknowledgments 215

A Testament to the Spirit

The second volume of Isaac Bashevis Singer's *Writings on Yiddish and Yiddishkayt* covers the years 1946 to 1955—the post-Holocaust period during which Singer's career began truly to take shape. During this period he wrote, edited, and collaborated on the translation of his first major novel, *The Family Moskat*, which appeared serially in Yiddish from 1945 to 1948 and was published in book form in both Yiddish and English in 1950. The English edition was published by Alfred A. Knopf, Inc., the same house that had published Israel Joshua Singer's major novels in English translation. But his older brother's experience was not replicated in Singer's case. He had made so many revisions during the translation process that the entire manuscript had to be retyped—at his own expense. And the translator, A. H. Gross, died before the translation was done, leaving his daughter, Nancy Gross, Maurice Samuel, Lyon Mearson, and Singer himself to complete the job. Upon its release it floundered both critically and commercially, leaving Knopf uninterested in Singer's other work.

Singer's English-language career was stagnant for another several years until a story he had first published in 1945, "Gimpl tam," was chosen for *A Treasury of Yiddish Stories* edited by Irving Howe and Eliezer Greenberg. They asked for translation help from Saul Bellow, who was credited as sole translator, and the story was published in 1953 as "Gimpel the Fool" in *Partisan Review*. This renewed attention to Singer's work likely led to the translation by Jacob Sloan of his first novel, *Satan in Goray*, and its publication by Cecil Hemley's Noonday Press at the end of 1955—an event prominently advertised for weeks in the pages of the Yiddish daily *Forverts*. In the meantime, Singer had written in Yiddish his epic prequel to *The Family Moskat*, *Der Hoyf* or *The Court*, which appeared much later as *The Manor* and *The Estate* in English. Unlike *The Family Moskat*, which had been largely ignored

by American literary critics, *Satan in Goray* was the first time that the *New York Times* reviewed a book by Isaac Bashevis Singer.

These, generally, are the broad brushstrokes of Singer's rise to literary prominence on the American literary scene during this period. What they fail to reveal, though, are the extremely powerful thoughts and emotions that drove Singer as a creative art-

An advertisement for Singer's novel in the *Forverts* in late 1955.

ist during this time. In these ten years Singer underwent a total transformation, reappraising everything he knew, questioning all his assumptions, and rebuilding both his artistic vision and his conception of what role literary artists played in the modern world.

This spiritual reappraisal was grounded in Singer's understanding of Yiddish language and literature within a broader perspective on Jewish history, culture, and religion. He turned to the world he knew most intimately—

the shtetl of prewar Poland—and mined it for every bit of spiritual content and inspiration he could retrieve. Sitting in New York, with the Cold War and McCarthyism gripping American hearts and minds, Singer dove deep into his own cultural and spiritual legacy—which had been under internal pressures since the arrival of the Haskalah, or Jewish enlightenment, in the early 19th century and was forever annihilated by external forces in the Holocaust.

The radical nature of Singer's literary and philosophical transformation during this period cannot be overstated. It comprised a total reevaluation of the foundations of Jewish life in the aftermath of World War II, accepting the facts on the ground while taking into account the forces of destabilization. Singer considered every circumstance in light of its spiritual implications. He examined each situation from the perspective of the human spirit. He was not merely interested in the social or political future of Jews in America, Israel, or other parts of the world. He was concerned about how they would find inspiration, joy, and meaning—not only as individuals but also as communities. Having been raised in a world where everything worked along sociocultural guidelines determined by religious life, and having himself witnessed the corrupting influence of self-interest on modern society, Singer undertook a concerted effort to distill the moral and social principles of the past into ideas that could be used in the present. He did more than offer people what David Roskies has called "a usable past"—a cultural history they can adopt as their own. He turned the raw material of the past into workable criteria that could be applied to build a viable future.

Singer's distillation of the Jewish past was motivated less by an intrinsic optimism than by frustration and disappointment in organized American Judaism—a circumstance evident in his repeatedly harsh criticism of Jewish movements, organizations, and institutions in America. The writings in this second volume reflect a process of increasing resignation to the fact that the institutional resources of various Jewish organizations were unlikely ever to prioritize the kind of creative and lively environment that Singer remembered existing in both the Polish shtetls and in Warsaw. His ideas for clubs, literary groups, or publishing enterprises that would be created and staffed by Yiddish writers and critics were apparently never taken up by those with the power to bring such projects to fruition. Singer's vision of "cultural democracy," which emphasized audience participation and experiential events, appears to have been largely ignored at the time of his writing. Yet these writings suggest that his growing bitterness merely sent him back to the page, where he worked out his ideas for the needs of the Jewish future in increasingly clear terms, projected them back onto the image of Old World Judaism, and filled those olden images with the dilemmas that were most pressing for people living in a post-Holocaust world.

The process of turning old-fashioned principles into new ideas involves a high degree of idealization—a necessary byproduct of Singer's broader project as it was shaped during this time in his life. While many of the facts he references may be accurate, not every detail he portrays has the meaning or significance he gives it in his writings. Neither does he always provide a full picture of the past. Singer's selective approach to portraying the shtetl and Jewish life is directly connected to the spiritual needs he identifies among people living in his own time. He is not merely reminiscing about what he saw during his childhood. He is using what he saw to give people meaning in the present. His descriptions and explanations cannot be read as objective portrayals of Jews in Eastern Europe. They must be read, as he himself writes in one of the later articles, with their *intention* in mind. Only when we understand Singer's intention, as laid out in his nonfiction, can we fully appreciate what he is doing in his fiction.

The most extraordinary aspect of this undertaking is that it was all laid out for readers in the pages of the *Forverts*, mostly under the pseudonym Yitskhok Varshavski. And while some readers likely wondered why this writer, who had so much to say about Yiddish literature and the Jewish world, published no literary work of his own, others surely made the connection. As time passed, it became increasingly difficult to separate Bashevis from Varshavski and Singer's other main pseudonym, D. Segal. An announcement on the paper's front page on July 8, 1955, said that the "famous author and *Forverts* writer Y. Bashevis" was leaving for a long trip to Europe and Israel, from which he would send articles and letters reporting on his travels. The announcement openly states: "From Europe, Y. Bashevis (who is also known to *Forverts* readers under his pen names Y. Varshavski and D. Segal) will travel to the State of Israel." The announcement also assured readers that Y. Bashevis's ongoing series, "In

My Father's Court," would continue to be printed each Saturday while he was away—though the series had only ever appeared under the name Varshavski.

Even readers who had not seen the first announcement might have noticed that as reports from Europe con-

An announcement for Singer's trip to Europe and Israel appearing in the *Forverts* on July 8, 1955

tinued to appear under the name D. Segal, another announcement on October 8, 1955, stated that "Yitskhok Bashevis is now in Israel" with a small box at the bottom reminding readers that "Bashevis signs his articles with the pen name D. Segal." The blurring line between these pseudonyms is represented in this collection by two pieces originally appearing under the name D. Segal—one of which was titled "At My Father's Courtroom" (November 25, 1954) and served as a pilot of sorts for the series of similarly titled vignettes, "In My Father's Courtroom," which first appeared on February 18, 1955. In the 1940s and early 1950s, these pseudonyms may have allowed Singer to publish different material under different identities, but as his literary star rose on both the American and Jewish cultural scenes, using different names became little more than a formality.

Singer took two trips to Europe in the ten years after the end of World War II—with one major difference between the two. In 1947, he traveled to England, France, and Switzerland, a trip that began with a visit to his older sister, Esther Singer Kreitman. Little is known of this trip in detail, yet, despite writing as Varshavski, Singer does describe his taxi turning onto his "sister's street" as he first arrives in London. He returned to New York in late November 1947, writing a piece titled "Europe Suffers a Spiritual Crisis" (December 3, 1947), and on February 22, 1948, Abe Cahan, the legendary *Forverts* editor, published a short critical piece on Kreitman's story "A Satin Coat,"

which had appeared a week earlier. Singer's likely role in bringing the story to the newspaper directly from London complicates the general impression that he did nothing to help his sister's literary career.

Singer's second trip to Europe, which also included his first to Israel, took place in the fall of 1955—just months after his reunion in New York with his son, Israel Zamir, whom he hadn't seen since leaving Poland twenty years

An announcement for Singer's arrival in Israel in the *Forverts* on October 8, 1955.

earlier. Zamir had come to New York as an emissary of Hashomer Hatzair, the Labor Zionist youth movement, meaning he was not in Israel, where he had grown up since 1938, when Singer embarked on his visit. In all, Singer's travels likely influenced his perspective on both the state of modern culture in the world and his own role as a Yiddish writer in America.

In many ways, the immediate post-Holocaust period of Singer's life culminated with the series that came to be known in English as *In My Father's Court*, describing his childhood as the son of a rabbi. This was a watershed moment for Singer as it integrated the main themes he was working to distill at the time—faith, intention, morality, personal philosophy—while applying what he set out as his own literary standard: arousing the inspiration of his readers by using his personal spark to ignite their internal fires. The series was the culmination of Singer's thinking over the decade that had passed since the end of World War II, recapturing the faith of his parents even if not returning to their traditional way of life. In his literary work, he achieved what he laid out theoretically in his essayistic writings: a consolidation of the past, present, and future in what appeared on the page as simple storytelling. At the outset of this process, just after World War II had ended, Singer was steeped in a mix of anger, protest, and readiness to fight for what mattered. During the ensuing years, he struggled with faith and doubt, returning repeatedly to his cultural roots to rediscover the sources that had propped up Jewish life for millennia. By the end of this internal process, he had reappraised the past to such an extent—excavating so much of what had given him and the people around him moral and spiritual strength—that he was ready to supply his own version of it in literary form.

In these pieces, Singer preaches a personal, idiosyncratic version of Jewish idealism. His vision for the survival of Yiddish is not merely practical but mainly spiritual: he wants to ensure not only that it will be *possible* to learn Yiddish but that people will *want* to learn it so they can gain access to its treasures. As he writes in "Our Language, Our People," an article published on the occasion of the first World Congress for Jewish Culture—a secular organization founded in September 1948 specifically to promote Yiddish culture throughout the world—the issue with Yiddish culture is one of quality. "The most crucial problems are how to maintain the Jewish spirit in a foreign environment," he wrote, "how to imbue our forms with greater Jewish content, how to exploit the spiritual goldmines that are hidden in the Yiddish language and Yiddish style. Our greatest danger is not the scarcity of numbers, but spiritual poverty." The path to preserving the legacy of Yiddish culture passed not through institutions but through the human spirit. And he repeatedly puts the burden for this to happen not on external efforts or circumstances but on the shoulders of writers themselves. If you wanted people to care about Yiddish, you had to give them something to care about.

Singer offers the clearest image of what Jewish idealism means to him in an article titled "Jews and the World" (November 22, 1952) where, for him, spirituality itself becomes a stand-in for what it means to be Jewish:

> Jews were not created to place all their hopes on human beings, on political flip-flopping, on this dubious world, on temporary victories. Jews have an internal fire that strives for eternity, for the lofty and the good, for the spheres that are not ruled by competition, lies, greed, contradictions, or falsities. If Jews had a corner where they could live spiritually, they wouldn't be so hot on the marketplace.

This may not reflect who Jews are in practice—it may not be a comprehensive portrayal of what being Jewish is all about—but it offers a lucid vision of what, for Singer, comprised Jewish spirit and principles. The notion of creating an earthly reflection of the heavenly realms was one of his most treasured qualities of Jewish spirituality, as he understood its history and intention.

Today, Singer's spiritual foresight seems nearly prophetic as the Jewish world, both in the diaspora and in Israel, undergoes its greatest crisis since the Holocaust. Some of the issues that Singer raises in this collection are not only prescient—they are more urgent in our day than they were in his. Singer's warning against the rise of dictatorships in societies that have lost faith in the rule of law reverberates deafeningly in the political climates faced by Jews in their two most populous locations, Israel and the United States. His call for a Jewish constitution—which would take the principles of the US Constitution as a baseline while adding clauses tailored to Jewish identity—seems like a missed opportunity for which all citizens of the State of Israel have paid with their nerves, civil rights, and national security. The corruption that has led to the greatest catastrophes since the founding of Israel was apparent to Singer in its earliest days as a potential threat. Where spiritual and communal significance are concerned, Singer's worries about the intentions motivating larger institutions and organizations continue to be all too real in a world increasingly structured by a monetized race for our attention and an illiberal centralizing of power.

In a sea of blockbusting and glory seeking, where intelligence is artificial and originality a failing commodity, Singer reminds us that the human spirit is our greatest treasure—and that we are each personally responsible for its safekeeping.

—*David Stromberg, Jerusalem*

Invoking Singer's characteristic iconoclastic style, this volume opens with a question rather than a declaration: What is the meaning of being Jewish after the Holocaust? In essence, he turns the Jewish question around and asks Jews themselves whether, having only partially survived an attempted annihilation, it is possible to clearly say what gives Jewish life purpose. With Jewish communities in Europe mostly destroyed, the push for Jewish self-determination in the Middle East gaining steam, American Jewry poised to enter mainstream society, and Jews in Muslim countries facing increasing harassment, Singer sets off on a conceptual and spiritual journey that will carry him through the coming decade. At this early point in the journey, he identifies the need for a purpose that will give Jewish life some direction as it reconstitutes itself from the greatest onslaught it has ever suffered.

The Eternal Jewish Question: What's the Purpose?
(January 15, 1946)

At no point since the Jews became a people has the problem of being Jewish been as critical as it is today. There are moments when it seems that almost all of the world's problems revolve around the Jewish question. We can say that the way one group or another relates to Jews is indicative of how it relates to all other questions. We have nearly become the testing ground for human thought and emotion.

But here we want to touch upon another topic. In no other time have Jews been such an enigma for themselves as they are today.

Our religious grandparents and great-grandparents had the answer to every question. They believed that the world was created for us, and so it was no wonder that other peoples of the earth were constantly fighting wars against us. Our forebears believed that the Jewish truth, our faith, would sooner or later rise like oil on water and that the promises of the prophets—that the Torah will go forth from Zion out to the whole world—had to come true. The Jewish religion found its own way to answer every difficult question.

Modern Jews—nonbelievers—find themselves in a completely different situation. In the simplest terms, we are nothing but a small, scattered group of people without a home, without a unifying language, and very often without faith. Many of today's Jews are Jewish merely because of their name and origin. They know nothing about being Jewish. They sometimes know less than learned Christians. A scattered, disjointed group such as this, which is also so small in numbers, should play no role. Yet, in reality, each of us feels that we have a great role to play.

Sure, our enemies all swear that we in actual fact control the world. We poison every nation, we hold influence over every government, we do whatever we want with the human species. Every full, half, or quarter antisemite is certain of these claims. They suggest that the world should set aside every other activity and concern itself with one: fighting the Jews. The fact that we are a negligible few makes no impression on them. They say that one single Jew can withstand a thousand non-Jews. Our enemies do everything they can to portray us as possessing a diabolical greatness, a mysterious power like nothing else that exists.

But not only our enemies—the few friends we have think this way too. Our defenders often point to our great spiritual value, our spiritual leadership. You could say that almost everyone agrees we have a great role to play, regardless of whether our role is considered benevolent or harmful.

At the same time there are millions of Jews who have not even begun to understand why we are supposed to be so important, what our role is actually, and why we've had so much publicity. Take, for example, Americanized young Jewish people in New York or Anglicized ones in London. They know very little about being Jewish. Quite often they haven't even peeped into the Hebrew Bible, let alone the Talmud or other religious books. They know no Hebrew and no Yiddish either. They don't feel like they have a mission in the world. The whole issue of being Jewish is nothing to them but a bundle of troubles. It stops them from getting accepted to university or landing a job at certain companies. Often, when such young people suffer due to their Jewishness, they ask themselves, "Why the devil am I carrying this burden? I don't care about the Jewish religion, and I'm not going to any Palestine either. Why not put an end to the whole comedy?" Some explain that they remain Jewish out of pride. Others say they try not to think about it. Still others admit that it's an ever-present enigma. They feel as if they suffer from an incurable illness. . . .

Yes, we are an enigma not only for the world but also for ourselves. Countless difficult questions arise as soon as you utter the word *Jewishness*. How long will it last? Why do people hate us? What role do we play? Are we a nation? A religion? A race? Internationalists? Can Palestine solve our problem? Or can socialism? Or both together? Or not even both together? You could ask and discuss without end.

The most crucial question is the question of secular Jews, those who are estranged. Their whole being asks, "Who am I? What do people want from me? How am I different from anyone else?"

I'd like to recall that our fathers and grandfathers also had a question that they often asked. The question was formulated in this way: "What's the purpose?"

This writer remembers that when he was a boy, his

uncle once stopped him in the middle of the street and asked, "Tell me, do you know the purpose of all this?"

"The purpose is that we're all going to die."

"That's the purpose?" asked his uncle, astonished.

"The purpose is that we'll get old and grow gray hair."

"That's not the purpose either!"

"What do you mean, Uncle? Earning a living? The world to come?"

"All of it! All of it!" his uncle yelled. "There has to be some purpose! We can't just live for the sake of it. We have to be redeemed. There has to be a great redemption of the world, both spiritual and material. There has to be some purpose!"

His uncle did not just speak but screamed. He waved his fist. Beneath his thick eyebrows, his eyes were on fire. It seemed as if his entire being was silently screaming, "I will not rest—and cannot rest—until there is some purpose!"

Interestingly, this writer has heard the same kind of speech, in various words and expressions, from all sorts of Jews. This writer is convinced that every Jew feels a sense of purpose. This is a feeling that things *should not* remain as they are. . . . Whether Jews want to make money or to bring about socialism, whether they want to fight for Palestine or send their children to Harvard University, the ideal of rising up always hovers before them—a sort of beauty or bliss that can't quite be put into words—arriving at some sense of purpose both in the material and the spiritual sense. Nothing is more painful to Jews than the thought that everything will remain as it is and that one day will be identical to the next. . . .

The concept of purpose is different from the concept of progress in that purpose has a thoroughly spiritual character. We can have progress in a technological sense and be stagnant in other domains. *Purpose* contains everything: personal happiness and the happiness of a people and of the world. It contains a powerful striving for spirituality, for loftiness, for a higher beauty. People who are governed by a purpose complex can never be content. They are always caught in a struggle. No matter what you give them, they will scream, "This isn't it!"

Our prophets cried out with powerful voices over two thousand years ago that it's impossible to live without purpose. This very cry boils in all our blood. Because of this very cry within ourselves, we can never really integrate with other nations.

Many estranged Jews are Jewish simply in that they are dissatisfied with themselves and with others—in that something constantly drives them to revolt. . . .

We keep driving both ourselves and others upward with a whip, even when the physical strength and the economic conditions are against it. No matter what other nations accomplish, we keep arguing, "Is that really the purpose? This is it?"

None other than Hitler declared that no system would ever satisfy the Jews. No matter what you give them, they will always cry that it's not enough, demanding more and more. Fascism was an attempt, once and for all, to shut the Jewish mouth, to cut out its tongue, which cries endlessly, "What's the purpose?"

This article in some ways expands on Singer's better-known essay "Problems of Yiddish Prose in America," appearing in 1943 in *Svive*, a Yiddish literary journal edited by poet and writer Kadya Molodowsky. Whereas the earlier essay called on modern Yiddish writers to draw on Jewish sources for both vocabulary and content, particularly religious books and commentaries, this article makes a case for drawing on ancient Jewish texts as stylistic models. Singer suggests that the specific dynamism of Jewish religious thinking offers a path toward a culturally informed literature that is distinguished from other literatures by its ties to its historical roots. These traditional sources, and not merely the literary achievements of the modern era, will help to produce a literature that is uniquely Jewish without undermining its value as contemporary writing.

On the Question of Style in Yiddish Literature
(February 10, 1946)

What exactly is a writer's style, or way of writing? What does it consist of? Do writers generally need to have a consistent writing style? Much ink has been spilled on all of these questions. Literary critics and professors have written large tomes on the topic. It's a fact that, with certain writers, a few sentences are enough to identify the author. Two lines are enough to recognize Shakespeare. The same is true of Heine, Goethe, Dostoevsky, and, in the case of our Yiddish writers, Mendele Moykher Sforim, Sholem Aleichem, and Y. L. Peretz. Tolstoy's style is not distinct enough to be identified within a couple of sentences, but two pages would certainly be enough for him to be recognized.

Sooner or later, anyone who studies literary style comes to the same conclusion: a writer's style expresses their character and personality. Just as people all have different faces, different voices, different handwriting, so they have their own manners of telling stories, of depicting things. One person speaks slowly, in a detailed way that's a little boring, another speaks quickly, nervously, cutting things short. One likes to relate stories for their own sake, without any purpose or sense, while another will only tell you something that's interesting. Some regularly use expressions that others use more rarely. Some say repeatedly, "Anyway, what was I saying? Oh yeah . . ."

Others say, "Not so fast! Hold on a minute . . ." And others speak haltingly, every couple of words sounding as if separate. Some like to preface everything with introductions. They line their stories with all kinds of caveats. All of these qualities turn up in a writer's style.

When you read Mendele Moykher Sforim, you get the sense that the writer is in no rush. He is certain that his readers are listening to him attentively. Reading Peretz, you often get the feeling that he's rushing and fearful of disturbing his readers. He wants to get to the point as quickly as possible. He doesn't reveal everything. He uses hints, insinuations. When it comes to Sholem Aleichem, dialogues and conversations play an important role. He lets his characters speak, and we learn everything from their words.

It's interesting that while writers each have their own styles, time periods have styles of their own too. Styles were created both by individuals and also by groups or generations as a whole. There's both a classic style and a romantic style. French and Russian realists write in different ways. In Russia, style still carries a collective quality. It still relates to the style of a generation, an epoch. People who lived during the same time period, in the same country, often have similar stylistic elements, though each of them has a different character. . . .

Jews have great hidden stylistic treasures that are rarely used. We are not only speaking here of Yiddish literature but of Jewish literature in general, both Hebrew and Yiddish.

The most recognizable Jewish style is the style of the Hebrew Bible. In the Torah we have the primary model for how a story should be told: short, to the point, with profound seriousness and blazing objectivity. The writer of these books loved Jacob and hated Esau, yet he described Jacob's tricks, how he fooled Esau out of his blessing and Laban out of his sheep. No matter who wrote the five books of Moses, you get the sense that it was a great and pure individual, someone with a noble character, a person who spoke the language of eternity—and who had truly earned immortality.

The Hebrew Bible features other styles. The prophets each had a language of their own. Books like Ecclesiastes, Job, and the Song of Songs vary greatly in their style and speech. Every one of them serves as its own model.

The style of the Mishnah is also quite interesting. It has, if you will, the same kind of gravity and seriousness as the Hebrew Bible. But it's also somehow different. There's a certain softness, a kind of lyricism, in the Mishnah's style. This is especially the case when it speaks of morals, of good traits, as in *Pirkei Avot*, the *Ethics of the Fathers*. The Mishnaic style is closer to today's Jews than the style of the Hebrew Bible.

Some Hebrew writers have tried using not only the Hebrew of the Mishnah but also its style, its form. The Mishnaic style is not sufficiently exploited in literature despite being an ideal form, a wonderful way of writing. Books are rarely as clear as the Mishnah. Every word is in just the right place. There's no flowery language, no repetition. Everything is described fully and precisely at once. True, the Mishnah is not a work of art, but rather a book of law. But its style can be used very well for art.

The style of the Gemara is rather strange. Actually, its Talmudic hair-splitting is so unique that nothing compares to it in all of literature. Thoughts aren't pursued in a straightforward manner. Rather, they are tossed here and there. Words are said and criticized on the spot. The analysis never stops. Each word presents a question and an answer. This unusual style has influenced not only religious judges and interpreters but also the entire Jewish way of thinking. It's like reading a literary work and a critical study of that work together with a discussion about the work and all kinds of research and conjectures that could only have been produced in relation to the work. Thoughts are never allowed to be completed but rather grab themselves by the hand. There's a lot of truth in the notion that Professor Freud's psychoanalysis is influenced by the Talmud. This doesn't mean that Freud studied the Talmud. The analytic way of thinking—the search in every word for different meanings, hints, deeper forces—is part of the Jewish mindset.

The style of the Aggadah, the stories told in the Talmud of things that relate purely to people's daily lives, has a particularly Jewish charm. The style of the Talmudic Aggadah as well as the Midrash, or interpretation, are deeply national—they reflect the entirety of the Jewish soul. In Aggadah, just as in Halakhah or religious law, there's none of the monotony, the repetitiveness, the tediousness of classic works by other peoples. Here too the thoughts work quickly, in a flash, like a zigzag. There's a story, then an interpretation. Here the writers are gravely serious, there they make a joke or even use rough language. The lyricism, storytelling, moralizing, and playfulness all go together. It's like in a Hasidic prayer house where one person studies and another tells a story, one drinks a glass of brandy and another recites the Kedushah prayer. This kind of blending has a distinctly Jewish flavor. Thoughts aren't congealed as in the monotonous Greek tragedies or even in Plato's *Dialogues*, where there's a sharpness of thought, but everything moves along in a single voice and in one direction. Diversity is characteristic of almost every Jewish style. Jewish thought can quickly pass from one subject to another, from one mood to the next.

This style has even expressed itself in the lively language used by Jews. When priests give a sermon, they grovel to their audience. You often hear the same words spoken repeatedly. When rabbis prepare a speech for Shabbat Ha'Gadol in the week before Passover, they do a little moralizing, work in some hair-splitting, offer up a parable, and while doing all this also talk about city affairs and community issues. It's not uncommon for them to make a joke too. Heine's style, in which lyricism and humor go together, is thoroughly Jewish. He is never too embarrassed, in the middle of a love poem, to laugh at love. He's religious at one point and heretical at another, now tender, and now biting.

While authors of Yiddish literature were learned—as knowledgeable as, say, Mendele, Sholem Aleichem, Peretz, or David Frishman—Yiddish literature was also diverse. This was especially apparent in Peretz's writing, which had everything mixed together. It spoke with a restless spirit that could, at the same time, both laugh and cry, joke around and preach, delve deeply into mysticism and also poke fun at the Kabbalah. But later, when Yiddish literature began very often to be written by crude, unlearned people, the style changed. It turned monotonous, syrupy, heavy, without zigzags. It seemed to suggest that we are a people like any other and that our literature had to go in the same direction as other literatures. But the truth is that the Jewish way of thinking has remained the same. Jewish readers often had no patience for this denationalized style. The Jewish palate likes pepper, salt, strong spices. It can't be nourished on greens alone, even if they're healthy. Let us say here that the same mistakes are made in Hebrew literature. They, too, want to introduce this denationalized monotony, this cold calm which leads to books that, while written in the holy tongue, have no Jewish flavor.

Yiddish literature has never been primitive. It was always sharp, varied, lyrical, thought-provoking, serious, funny, realistic, romantic—all at once. It has reflected the Jewish spirit not in a congealed manner, but rather in motion, in its coming into being. The heavy mind, like the heavy hand, does not suit Yiddish literature, which has always had wings.

In this article, Singer begins to delve into one of the themes that would preoccupy him for the rest of his career: the minds and hearts of Holocaust survivors. Yet he also begins laying out the worldview that he would develop in countless works of fiction—that, religion aside, people need to believe in something in order to live. It can be socialism or Zionism or capitalism, but some expression of faith lives in people regardless of their experiences. In this case he expresses his own belief—against all odds and barely a year after the end of World War II—that Jews, as a people without a land, will establish a state because their struggle is just. Notably, he does not suggest that the Holocaust proves the need for a Jewish state. Rather, he points out that the fact that Jews returned from the hell of near annihilation with their faith intact is itself proof of their belief in themselves as a nation.

They Were in the Nazi Hell and Still Did Not Lose Their Faith in Humanity

(July 1, 1946)

Things often happen in a way that's different from what everyday logic would dictate. This is especially true in Jewish life.

In recent months, Jews from Poland and Germany have begun to appear, the last remnants of the Holocaust. Those of us who were here had expected them to be completely spent, so full of despair that it would be impossible to talk to them.

In reality, the people who came are quite interested in life and are often full of humor. They do not want to play the role of heroes or martyrs. Naturally, they admit that the Jewish situation is desperate, but they themselves don't want to carry the marks of the Holocaust on their faces. Many of them could even practically be called optimists.

Religious Jews do not argue with God. They have the same old answer: this is God's will and we have to accept His decrees. These Jews continue to pray, calling God the Father of Mercy, though they know all too well that this "merciful father" looked on silently as children were buried alive, sending forth no miracles.

The socialists continue to talk about socialism and about the brotherhood of the nations and of the masses, though they themselves witnessed how the masses were slaughtered, tortured, and robbed by men whose consciences were at peace.

The Zionists continue to believe in the Land of Israel though they know that Palestine is in the hands of the English, who do everything possible for us not to raise our heads there. Simple reasoning says that the English and the Arabs will be the victors, not the small number of Jews.

When we look at these people, we come to the conclusion that changing a person's faith is just as difficult as changing their physical appearance. It happens that people get disappointed or change their beliefs, just as it happens that a nose breaks or a head of hair goes bald. But generally our convictions sit firmly in our minds. No matter how terrible our experiences may be, they don't alter our attitudes.

We realize this when we look at the Nazis, the Germans, too. Everyone who has returned from Germany has admitted that a great number of the German people are ready at any moment to follow a new Hitler. The millions of Germans who believed in Germany above all else believe in it still—regardless of Germany having lost two world wars and the Germans having turned into naked beasts. . . .

The writer of these lines has no access to the minds of other people, but he knows more or less what's happening in his own mind. This writer is convinced that Jews should have Palestine and believes that have it they will. Every day this belief takes a new hit. This writer suffers when he reads that the Arab states all stand against the few Jews of the Land of Israel. It angers him when he learns that the English Labor Party and Conservative Party, which represent 90 or more percent of the English people, support the Bevin Plan. Tens of millions of Arabs and tens of millions of English people are a colossal power. Logic dictates that such power will prevail. But this writer will not give up. His reason is this: justice is on our side. We Jews must have a country just like every other people. . . .

In the last analysis, for all people, the truth consists of whatever they think will make them, their group, their people, or their class greater and stronger. Lies consist of whatever tries to destroy them or their group.

The nationalist egoism of the German people dictated that Germany could exist only if its neighbors were destroyed. Germany has believed in this truth for a long time now. Many Germans believe that though Hitler has lost the war, he has done the German people a great favor by killing millions of its neighbors. This will be useful during World War III. The idea that Germany needs to conquer large territories, especially in the east, has been pounded into the German mind like a nail. If you want to get rid of the nail you have to chop off the head of the beast.

In our Jewish minds, too, sits an idea that won't leave us. It's the thought that we were, are, and will always remain a nation—which is why we need our own country. The number of Jews against this idea gets only smaller. . . .

We know too little of human history, too poorly the ways and aims of nature, to determine which kinds of truths will win out and what nature is striving toward in general terms. But we know enough about history to say that many great kingdoms with large appetites and the conviction that the entire world was created just for them became, with time, smaller and smaller.

It's not yet out of the question that the entire human race will, sooner rather than later, have to renounce its sense of pride. Isaiah prophesied long ago that there will come a day when human greatness will be lowly and bent over. But until that day, that part of the human race whose truth is *all for me and none for others* will most likely experience bitter disappointment. The fact that we Jews, the smallest of the small, have outlived so many giants suggests that our faith may be closer to some absolute truth than the faith of strength and violence.

The faith of the Jews who have made it back from the Nazi hell shows that our truth cannot be shattered by any brutal power.

Whereas in other articles Singer speaks of good and evil in mystical or historical terms, here he returns to moral terms as set out in the Hebrew Bible—particularly as concerns the question of free choice. He frames this issue around human relationships and the need for ethical behavior despite the human tendency toward corruption and sloth. Yet Singer also notes that Jewish philosophy does not strive for a human system of government or control that would wipe out all evil. This, he argues, would undermine what he calls the divine source of free choice. In the real world, he argues, there will always be evildoers—because human nature is designed in such a way that being good means choosing to be good.

The Philosophy of Our Prophets

(March 1, 1947)

The worldview of the Hebrew Bible is expressed in the idea that there is a single God who, out of an internal free will, created the heavens, the earth, and all living creatures. God is just, good, and merciful. God emanates no evil. If we nevertheless see bad things happening, this is because we don't know God's ways—because divine thought is as far from ours as the heavens are from the earth.

Jews share this first part of the Hebrew Bible's philosophy with many others from both ancient periods and modern times. Then comes the second and very important part of its philosophy, which is expressed in the idea that humanity finds itself in a special and significant position. As opposed to all other objects and creatures, which behave according to their natures, humankind has been given freedom. People can choose between good and evil, between life and death. They have the power of choice.

The ability to choose between good and evil makes humankind a very privileged sort of creature, but it also provides the opportunity to be hateful and depraved. Through their actions, people can raise themselves to the levels of the prophets, reaching spiritual heights, or they can be the greatest lowlifes, beings that bring forth only injury, darkness, and sorrow. We have the power to choose between the two.

Nature is created such that people always find themselves at a crossroads. Every minute they stand before two choices: to do good or bad. Everything connected with the human species lies in the spheres of good and bad. There's no neutral zone. Either we fulfill a commandment or we commit a sin.

If commandments were rewarded and sins were punished on the spot, there would be no free choice. People would soon see that it served them to be righteous rather than wicked, and free choice would come to an end.

But since God wanted choice to exist, God waits both with reward for commandments and also with punishment for sins. It's true that there are rewards and punishments, but they are doled out in such a way that people are left to question what serves them best, doing good or doing evil. God's mills grind slowly. Only good-willed people understand that it's better to be on the side of good than on the side of evil. Immoral people tend to deny reward and punishment. They reckon not with long-term experience but with the current moment. It's true that in general crime doesn't pay, but criminals don't see this truth. On the contrary, they see that when you have a successful holdup, you bring in easy money. If all criminals were caught on the spot, as soon as they committed their first crime, there would be no criminals, and there wouldn't be any free choice either. So for choice to exist, the wicked have to succeed from time to time. There even have to be wrongdoers who live out long happy years. Because if *every* wrongdoer, without exception, came to a hateful end, this again would reduce free choice.

Since God's mill grinds so slowly, there will always be righteous and wicked people. And more: there will always be entire groups that will choose between good and evil. . . .

Of what does the good path consist? The more you study the Hebrew Bible, the more you see that almost all good deeds are connected with relationships between people. The quintessence of every good deed is: don't harm your neighbors. Do them good. The religious law to keep Shabbat is connected with giving rest to the slaves, servants, oxen, and donkeys. The reason given for why we should rest on Shabbat is the fact that we were ourselves slaves. Don't steal, don't commit murder, don't covet someone else's wife, ox, donkey, or property. Don't swear falsely and don't bear false witness. In short, don't harm other people's bodies or property. Many times the Hebrew Bible repeats that God wants justice above all. This is the main issue. People who are righteous don't steal or rob from others, they don't take bribes, they're good to orphans and widows and hired workers, they judge fairly and speak the truth. Wrongdoers are those who do the opposite. You could say that wicked people are those who want something for nothing. The righteous want nothing for free. They're ready to pay for everything. On the contrary, they are ready to help others who can't support themselves through work.

Why did the Hebrew Bible put so much emphasis on this point? The answer is that all temptations revolve around this issue. You can get anyone to take part in all kinds of ceremonies, sacrifice offerings, wear special garments, adopt all kinds of customs. But it's very hard to get people not to seek privileges for themselves. The human desire to get something for nothing is frighteningly powerful. Everyone wants to find a good bargain in life. They want to get rich on someone else's dime, make love with someone else's wife, be respected on someone else's account—they're always trying to grab something or get something. This is what humanity strives for under all circumstances, every social system. Thieves, robbers, scammers, moochers, false prophets, flatterers, informers, gossipers, racists, bribers, liars, speculators, exploiters, false witnesses, intriguers, glory seekers—they all have one goal: getting something for nothing. This is what divides people into good and evil. This is where the paths of good and evil split. One path is godly. The other leads to the abyss.

Good people have always tried to create systems that would make privilege, exploitation, and evil impossible. But according to Jewish philosophy, humanity will never bring about a system that brings an end to free choice. People will be able to do evil under any system. If there were ever a system that made evil impossible, where every sort of exploitation would be punished, it would bring an end to free will, to choice. It's good that people want to improve the world, but the Hebrew Bible proclaims in advance: "There will never cease to be needy people in this world." There will always be wrongdoers and those who are wronged, though the wrongs will be done under different pretexts, under the most different circumstances. Wrongdoing will only end when free choice comes to an end and humanity is redeemed: when wolves lie with sheep and bring forth offspring.

Yes, redemption has to come sooner or later, but it will only arrive when good finally becomes stronger than evil. These two sides, the virtuous and the villainous, fight an ancient battle. They are both powerful forces. They both have their own arguments, their own philosophies. Wicked people are wise in their evildoing. They know all the tricks.

In contrast to the New Testament, which preaches that we should be silent in the face of evil and let ourselves be trampled by the wicked, the Hebrew Bible tells us to wage a fierce battle against evil. The Hebrew Bible warns us about clearing away evil and destroying the wicked every chance we get. Righteous people have to be active. They have to wage God's war. If they don't, wrongdoing will inundate everything, as it did in Sodom and Gomorrah. Righteous people can await God's help to arrive sooner or later, but only when they make their greatest efforts, when they've used up *all* their strength.

The Jewish people have an ancient covenant with God. It has countless times stood on the side of good. But it has also sinned many times, and God is stricter with the people of Israel than with other nations because Jacob was God's slave. It is their responsibility to stand at the very front of the war between good and evil. The reward that God promises the Jewish people is that they'll triumph in the end. Jacob will return to his land. The Torah will go forth from Zion and become a light unto the nations.

It is natural for Jewish philosophy to put all responsibility on humankind. The New Testament excuses the wicked by telling them that they don't know what they're doing. There are many philosophers who have altogether discarded the idea of free choice. Jewish philosophy is built on free will. This is the foundation of the Jewish people.

There is no solution for humanity. People can't depend on any social system or circumstances. They are obliged to be good in *every* system, under *all* circumstances. Before they try to make others good they themselves have to be good.

The Hebrew Bible demands "not a lot" from people: honesty. But the truth is that you can't ask for more. This is where you really see people. This is where the greatest slip up. This is where entire peoples and generations fall. This is where, day in and day out, people face temptation: choosing between life and death, good and evil.

People have pummeled this philosophy from different sides. They've called it false, barbaric, cruel, primitive. But it has remained standing like a fortress wall. Every true moral is held up by it. Every fair law draws from its source. It's a philosophy that's confirmed by experience at every step. We see how not only individual people but entire groups are corrupted. We see how strong temptations can be—on a daily and even hourly basis.

President Roosevelt has proclaimed that the world should be built on the principles of the Ten Commandments. The trouble is that such a world can never fully be built. Thieves, robbers, liars, and those who try to take what belongs to others will always have their chance to get things. There cannot exist a world *without choice*.

This is the tragedy of humankind—but also its greatest potential.

In this article, written less than three years after the end of the Holocaust, Singer was already warning against the cheapening of its meaning. Continuing his preoccupation with Holocaust survivors, it appeared just weeks after his first trip to Europe since leaving Poland in 1935—during which he traveled to England, France, and Switzerland—and reflected his meetings with Jews still living on the other side of the Atlantic. As his frame, he uses the religious fast day known as Tisha B'Av, during which Jews mourn the destruction of the Temple in Jerusalem as well as other catastrophes that befell the Jewish people during their centuries of exile. This link is made more powerful by the Yiddish word for the destruction of the Temple, *khurbn*, the same word used to refer to the Holocaust.

Jewish Tragedy Should Not Be Made Mundane

(January 17, 1948)

Jews have recently gotten into a very disheartening habit. They've started overusing our greatest destruction—the six million who perished in Europe during the Holocaust.

Our parents and grandparents had only one day a year when they lamented the destruction of the Temple. They fasted, turned benches over so as not to sit on them, took off their shoes, grieved. Rivers of tears were spilled during Tisha B'Av. Our parents' grief was so great that many of them fell sick from crying and wailing. This led the rabbis to permit making jokes and lifting people's spirits up a little. This is why we throw burrs and thistles at cantors as they recite Lamentations. You do it the next day too.

Many religious Jews who wanted to grieve over the destruction of the Temple more than once a year would wake up after midnight to study and pray in its memory. They studied half the night, smeared ash on their foreheads, and quietly cried about the destruction of the Temple and the fact that the *Shekhinah*, God's female presence, went into exile. This was all done quietly. It was a hidden practice.

Jews today are quite far from this kind of sadness. Even during the worst of the slaughters, we never stopped with the anniversaries, banquets, celebrations. We can't complain about this. Our hearts were hardened. Our egoism grew strong. We couldn't help ourselves. Compared with our parents we acted as if we weren't Jewish at all.

But it would be much better if we had at least the strength to be silent, at least to not play down our tragedy—to not belittle it or use it to serve our own interests or as a form of entertainment. Unfortunately, we can't bring ourselves to stop. The six million Jews have become a literary topic.

The poets can't stop writing odes to Treblinka, Majdanek, and Auschwitz. We put on plays about the Holocaust. The destruction of the Jewish people is being exploited in the most disparate ways. Jewish singers and actors in the middle of their acts rattle off a song about the six million. Not long ago this writer met a girl who studies at a Yiddish-English Sunday school. The teacher told her to compose a dramatic piece for her and for the other children to act out. She read aloud part of what she'd written. It was about a train filled with Jews being led to the incinerators. A child jumped off the train. Nazis shot at him. It goes without saying that the piece was beyond help. What can you expect from a kid? I looked at the girl. There was not a trace of sadness on her face. She read the story like something from *A Thousand and One Nights*. There's no point in blaming the child. It's her teachers and parents who've turned something that should be holy into something cheap and mundane. It would be good to tell such Jews that you don't let kids write plays about trains heading to Auschwitz.

A number of fundraisers also use the six million to raise money. First they talk about Jewish misfortune.

Then they pull out their alms box. We'd like to state that no matter how important the cause, this is no way to soften the hearts of those who might contribute. If we start describing the gas chambers every chance we get, it will turn the whole thing into an everyday issue. After a while, it will stop working altogether, and anything that's said will simply become an insult to the victims. Even when we collect money to help Jews in displaced-persons camps, we don't have to tell the whole story over again. Words like *Auschwitz*, *Treblinka*, and *Majdanek* should not be uttered with a light heart, at every opportunity, or for every cause. When it comes to certain things, silence is best.

We all experience different kinds of tragedies in our personal lives. Those closest to us die. We have all kinds of disappointments. But no one wants to be reminded of them all the time. Each tragedy needs its own surrounding stillness. We shouldn't make a lot of noise about things that demand the greatest spiritual questioning, the deepest quietude.

Not long ago this writer was invited to someone's house along with about a dozen other Yiddish writers. What do you think they did? They ate, drank wine, and chatted about Nazis, Auschwitz, murders, saintly victims. Can you imagine religious Jews getting together for a festive meal and talking for hours about the destruction of the Temple? No, those Jews knew that each activity had its time. You talk about the destruction of the Temple on Tisha B'Av, by candlelight, on benches that are turned over. When you put on satin caftans and sit down to a festive meal, you keep quiet about the destruction of the

Temple. And then it's much more pleasant to sing a little tune or do a little dance. Those Jews had good form. They had a sense of timing.

We modern Jews have lost all our traditions. We're ruled by a terrible sense of confusion. We mix everything up together: Tisha B'Av, Simhat Torah, Purim. Our actors sing about love at one moment and at another they recite, "Merciful God!" At one moment they clown around and use obscenities, and at another they praise the heroes of the ghettos. This is all done without connection to anything, and naturally it doesn't make much of an impression on the public. They can sense that it's nothing but theatrics.

Words need their own place, their own atmosphere. In *Dos pintele yid*, a play about "the Jewish spark," lots of noble things are said about the eternal nature of our people, about our dedication to Jewish life, about our struggle for justice. Yet we consider it a trashy play. It's trashy because these lofty words have been mixed up with old jokes, silly dances, all kinds of senseless scenes and sayings. We are now in danger of cheapening the destruction of a great part of our people.

What would our brothers and sisters from Poland have said had they seen how people exploit their misfortune? They would surely not have believed it.

This writer returned from Europe not long ago. He met Jews who had themselves been in the ghettos and fought the Nazis. We spent time with these Jews, ate and drank with them. There were lectures. But during the whole time not a single word was uttered about the destruction of Poland. This writer met a young poet who had spent two years with his wife hiding in a closet. Shereshevski, the poet, sat with his wife at the table speaking, listening, and asking questions about America. But they were silent about those terrible moments. It's completely natural to these writers that such moments should be considered holy. If you do talk about them, it's at the right time and in the proper atmosphere. I spent hours in Paris with Benn, a well-known Jewish painter, and only when I was about to leave his house did I incidentally discover that he and his wife had lived for a long period in the dark basement of this very building, sitting out every minute in fear of being denounced to the Nazis. The artist talked about every topic except this one.

Every Jew you meet in Paris is the hero of a frightful drama. Every one of them is alive because of some miracle. But none of them talk about it. Generally speaking, people who are affected deeply by things tend to stay quiet. Our local talkativeness is quite dubious. Yiddish poets, journalists, social organizers, actors, and anyone speaking in public should be very careful not to make light of what's holy to us. The six million dead are not a topic for poetry, plays, songs, or any other form of entertainment. The most beautiful words can turn ugly when not uttered in the right environment and without an inner shiver.

This article appeared on the prominent Literature page of the Sunday *Forverts*'s Second Section devoted to the inaugural World Congress for Jewish Culture, an organization known in Yiddish as the *Alveltlekher Yidisher Kultur-kongres*, which continues to exist today. The special feature included an article titled "The Goals of the Congress for Jewish Culture" by Yiddish writer and Jewish labor movement leader Nathan Chanin, known in Yiddish as Nokhum Khanin; an article titled "A Blessing in Jewish Life" by writer, journalist, and editor Dr. Zvi Cahn; and a poem titled "Lament in *Mame-loshn*" by poet Mani Leyb. It is notable that despite being featured alongside such recognizable figures on such a significant occasion, Singer nevertheless published the piece under the byline of Yitskhok Varshavski, the same pseudonym under which most of his critical writing appeared. Regardless, even at this unique moment, he took the opportunity to reiterate two of his main guiding points about the future of Yiddish literature: that it has to draw from traditional and religious sources, and that it has to worry less about quantity than about quality.

Our Language, Our Literature

(September 19, 1948)

When people's lives don't go smoothly, their problems grow. You meet people for whom things go so wrong that everything becomes a problem. Eating becomes a problem. Getting dressed becomes a problem, and going out of town to your summer home is also a problem. There's a Yiddish saying: no matter how you lay sick people out, it hurts them.

Recently, Jewish life has developed in such a way that we are practically millionaires when it comes to problems. No matter where we go we come up against difficulties. The simplest things have become complicated and full of contradictions. One such phenomenon today is Yiddish language and Yiddish literature.

For most people it's a given that an ethnic group has a language and a literature. In our case the whole thing stands under a question mark. Is Yiddish really our language? Could Yiddish be used in today's America to conduct business, work, and study? Can there be talk of any formal literature when the number of readers grows smaller from day to day and when the younger generation is raised in English? Recently there's been new trouble: a number of Yiddish authors have begun suffering greatly from the uprootedness that is characteristic of Jewish America. Books appear that are both Yiddish and also not Yiddish. The language is somehow very far from our mother tongue, our *mame-loshn*. Somehow the sentences are not structured in a Yiddish manner. The content itself is somehow foreign, as if it were translated from another language. You sometimes get the same feeling even when you peruse a book with many Hebrew quotes and famous names from Jewish history. You read, let's say, an article or a poem about the Vilna Gaon or the Baal Shem Tov, but somehow it doesn't talk about these great figures in a Jewish way. The words of praise appear exaggerated and awkward. The whole way in which these figures are conceived is not in our style. It seems to have been transposed from English. It feels as if someone who isn't Jewish has learned a little about our sacred texts and begun talking about our personal matters. It lacks any Jewish flavor.

These kinds of works inspire more fear in this writer than does the fact that the number of readers only gets smaller, or that young people are not getting a Yiddish education. We got used to scarcity a long time ago. And in our history, there's nothing new about assimilation either. The main thing is for the spiritual core to remain. Every time we have been destroyed, it left behind a new Yavne—the city of scholars who would not allow the Jewish spark to be extinguished after the destruction of the Second Temple. As long as Yiddish can carry a genuine Jewish spirituality within itself there is no danger of Yiddish writing becoming a lone voice in the desert. Yiddish literature would have to be translated into Hebrew and other languages. Jewish students would learn Yiddish specifically to be able to do research and understand Yiddish books. Yiddish would endure—if not as the language of daily life then as the intimate tongue of Yiddishkayt. There were always, as there are now too, chances that in the diaspora, Yiddish would take the place of what was once the Holy Tongue. In a certain sense, this is already the case today. Many Jewish readers purchase Yiddish newspapers not to learn about news in general but rather specifically for news in Yiddish. Theatergoers don't attend the Yiddish theater to see just any play—they want to see a *Yiddish* play. If they send their children to a Yiddish school, it's not to learn general subjects but specially to learn Yiddish.

Let's tell it like it really is: Creating a secular Yiddish culture in the fullest sense of the word is impossible in America. Yiddish can only exist here as a language that serves our Jewish needs. Yiddish is no longer the language we speak on the streets, in the factories, when we do business or study at university. It increasingly becomes a medium for conveying our unique Jewish sentiment and thought. Anyone talking about Yiddish culture has to reckon with this fact. Those who ignore this truth will be entangled in a web of endless mistakes.

As soon as this is the case, the issue of Yiddish culture is mainly a problem of quality. Sure, it would be better for Yiddish books to be circulated than it would for them to sit on the shelf. It would certainly be good for more schools to be established. But we cannot count too much on such efforts. We have to accept in advance that the number of Jews who will actually need a Jewish language of their own will be limited. Yiddish authors must be and must remain idealists. There is no other justification for their toils. The most crucial problems are how to maintain the Jewish spirit in a foreign environment, how to imbue our forms with greater Jewish content, how to exploit the spiritual gold mines that are hidden in the Yiddish language and in the Yiddish style. Our greatest danger is not the scarcity of numbers but spiritual poverty. Yiddish will die only when assimilation penetrates us from *within*—when our language gets watered down, our thoughts disjointed, our style corrupted. The rise of Yiddish during the late 1800s and early 1900s did not consist in our then having great numbers of readers or theatergoers but rather in our having a Mendele Moykher Sforim, a Sholem Aleichem, a Y. L. Peretz. There may even be more Yiddish schools and books today than there were in 1904 or 1912.

It isn't hard to persuade Jewish people to buy a Yiddish book or magazine. But it gets harder to offer such readers the kind of spiritual nourishment that will inspire them to buy another book or another periodical. As Americans say, you can lead a horse to water, but you can't make it drink. Let's not be ashamed of admitting the truth. Readers in 1904 and 1912 were excited by their reading material. It gave them spiritual pleasure. Today's readers are usually disappointed. Our literature no longer warms the Jewish heart. Most of what our journals publish is cold, fake, random. The language has become stale. This writer is himself an old reader of Yiddish literature and feels the coldness blowing from today's Yiddish authors. We should add that every rule has an exception and that we don't intend to offend anyone. But no illness can be healed without a proper diagnosis.

What are the reasons for this coldness? Why did one

period produce so much genuine Yiddish talent while now we are experiencing such lean years? And most important: What can we do to heal this spiritual malnutrition?

Our earliest authors were deeply rooted in our way of life and in our old literature. Mendele, Sholem Aleichem, and Peretz were all steeped in the very brine of Jewish life, and they were all learned. Every one of them knew every little corner of Jewish life and creativity. Regardless of whether a book by one of these authors was more or less successful, you never encountered any sense of alienation in them. Whether Sholem Aleichem wrote a brilliant story or simply let his pen go and scribbled something, it always had a particular Jewish charm. His authenticity issued from every line. He was thoroughly one of us.

Sustaining such authenticity is no simple thing when you've been uprooted from the old country for decades and, to top it off, have acquired less knowledge. It's not enough to read a story from a religious book and then, the next day, turn it into a novel or short story or even a poem. No matter how much we want to conceal this uprootedness and patch it over with religious rules or quotes, it comes off slipshod. Yiddish writers in America—and in other countries as well—suffer from an illness that's progressing slowly but surely. We are being eaten by a microbe that drains the marrow from our bones. We forget the old ways we lived, but we don't have the language or the forms to portray the new way of life that has developed here—a life for which our Yiddish language is inadequate. The Holocaust has invaded the very center of our Yavne. We can say that at no other time have the spokespeople of Yiddish been as bewildered and helpless as we are here in America. On top of these troubles, we are also trying to deny this illness to ourselves and to others, creating new neuroses. We are very sensitive to opinions. We keep holding all kinds of anniversaries and award celebrations. We have become unhealthily energetic and active. We worry that, after us, everything will be finished, and we look for old-time cures or magic potions to turn our situation around.

The truth is that only one sole cure exists: *religious study!* It's a cure that's as old as the Jewish people: *ve'hagita bo yomam va'layla*—"and you shall study by day and by night." Judaism has always consisted of religious study. When the author of the first chapter of the Psalms wanted to portray someone as righteous, they said that they studied by day and by night. It's hard to know what exactly Jews studied in ancient times, but the fact is that they studied—that religious study was their ideal. No one has yet written the great work that would demonstrate the colossal role that religious study has played in the development of the Jewish people. The words *Am Ha'Sefer*, "The People of the Book," express the essence of Jewishness.

If religious study was so necessary when Jews lived in their own land, or in different Jewish neighborhoods throughout the diaspora, where they led strictly religious lifestyles, we can only imagine how necessary it is here in America, where there is almost no religious discipline and where we are attacked by foreign spiritual powers from all sides. Here, a Jew without religious books is no longer a Jew. It can be boldly said about us that *eyn lanu shiyur ela ha'Torah ha'zot*—we have nothing left but studying Torah.

Yiddish literature can exist in America only if Yiddish authors cling tooth and nail to our spiritual inheritance. You can't force Yiddish readers into a state of *torato umanuto*, turning religious study into a profession. But for Yiddish writers there is surely no other way. No matter how much Yiddish writers know, they know too little. Here we have to know more than Mendele, Sholem Aleichem, and Peretz because we don't have the kind of contact with the simple people that they had. We have to become great experts of Yiddish language and Yiddish style. We have to study the Hebrew Bible and the Talmud, the Kabbalah and Hasidism, religious philosophy and the *Shulhan Arukh*, Rabbi Joseph Karo's book of religious law—and all this on top of needing to be familiar with modern Hebrew and Yiddish literature. For Yiddish to not be forgotten we have to take upon ourselves the same work that the YIVO Institute for Jewish Research in Vilna took upon itself: collecting and recording everything that has to do with the Yiddish language and its idiomatic expressions. Yiddish writers have to hone their instruments just as Bialik and other Hebrew writers have honed theirs. The truth is that Yiddish writers have to know Hebrew and Hebrew writers have to know Yiddish. Both of these languages are, in fact, two sides of the very same coin.

We often talk about the fact that there is no new generation of Yiddish writers growing. Such a generation will never grow if we don't raise it. We need to create a sort of seminary or studyhouse which will raise young people who are ready to dedicate their lives to Yiddishkayt. This writer is sure that we could find a couple dozen young people in America who are ready to sit and spend ten or fifteen years on religious study. If such an institution were put in good hands, it could prepare the right spiritual leaders for the coming generation. We can obviously have no guarantee that these students will have any talent for writing. But when such an institution gets to be known, it gradually attracts creative forces to itself. The institutions that have been created in today's America have two short-comings. First, they don't teach enough. Students from most of the yeshivas and Jewish colleges in America leave with superficial knowledge. Second, they don't study Yiddish, and without Yiddish, no one can be a true spiritual leader, neither in the lands of the diaspora nor in Israel.

When we talk about religious study together with creative writing, we must not forget the crucial role that criticism has always held for Jews. Even our holiest values are critiqued. The Talmud is filled with disagreements between Tannaic and Amoraic sages, questions and answers that are, in reality, critiques. The Torah interpreters were actually the first Bible critics, in the best sense of the word. We have in recent years greatly neglected this field of inquiry. Too often our criticism gets bogged down in empty acclaim and petty politics. But this has nothing to do with the subject of criticism. More than all other literatures, Yiddish literature requires an honest guide and a thorough analysis. For criticism to be useful, it would be good for writers to read their works to each other or for critics to revise and improve writing even before it gets published. Fear of criticism is the same as fear of learning. It's a telltale sign of stagnation. It does not need to be said that false criticism brings only harm.

In this writer's opinion, our contemporary Yiddish literature is a victim, in part, of false and tasteless criticism.

The idea of this article is that the biggest problem of Yiddish and Yiddish literature lies not in numbers but in quality. It is by far not a question of how many books we disseminate, how many schools we build, or how many kids will go there but mainly what books will be written and what will the schoolkids study. The same can be said of the theater. One good genuinely Yiddish play is worth more than something with shock value, created partly by the writer and partly by the director, just to get through the season. One thoroughly prepared lecture is more important than a series of speeches given on random topics that chew the same old straw. The policy of offering everything in little smatterings will never lead to success. It will not cure ignorance, it will not prevent assimilation. We'd do better to concentrate on those few for whom Yiddishkayt is the main focus. Let's prepare the best possible for them. Slowly but surely, quality will lead to quantity and greater numbers too.

In this article, Singer returns to one of his eternal themes—the paradox of modern Jewishness—this time from the perspective of faith, a topic that increasingly gained significance for him in the decade following the Holocaust. He frames the paradox as an internal conflict and suggests that the only way to move past this tension is through the phenomenon of faith, which functions regardless of people's religious adherence. He notes that every human activity—religious, political, cultural, social, economic—demands a measure of faith in higher powers, and that most of the people who deny such powers themselves doubt their own convictions.

Modern Jews and Their Internal Conflict

(November 27, 1948)

There's a difficult question that all modern Jews ask themselves sooner or later: If I don't believe that God gave the Torah on Mount Sinai, why should I bother with Jewishness? How is American culture any worse than Jewish culture? What is Jewishness in the first place when there's no faith?

This question is as old as the period of Jewish Emancipation and Enlightenment. This question is asked by both the assimilationists and by those who are still connected to Jewish culture. You sit at a meeting where people are discussing putting up a building for a Yiddish theater and you ask yourself: Why is a Yiddish-language theater any better than an English-language theater? What's the difference between watching a comedy in one language or another? Since there's no belief in the world to come or in the Messiah, why are we so vehemently against assimilation?

We ask ourselves this question consciously and we ask it even more often in our unconscious. This question often sabotages our actions because there's nothing more disturbing than an internal conflict. When things are not done with a full heart and with clear convictions, they never turn out as they should. This is, in this writer's opinion, the main reason we keep doing and doing things, and everything remains as it was.

According to Freud's theory, an internal conflict can only be healed when you bring it out of its hiding place and make it clear. The deeper the conflict is hidden, the more damage it does. So let's analyze ourselves—our own thoughts and our actions.

There's no doubt that in every modern Jew there lies hidden a bit of an assimilationist. We ourselves, the older ones, may move heaven and earth to build up Jewish culture. But we're raising our children so that they can find their place among our non-Jewish neighbors. At best, we teach them a smattering of Yiddish or Hebrew. There's an ethics book, *Behinot Olam* or *Aspects of the World*, written by Rabbi Yedaya Hapnini, which says, "Children are the secrets in their parents' hearts." In other words, parents raise their children to be what they themselves wish they were. If we raise our children to be doctors, lawyers, or engineers, it's because that's what we ourselves wanted to become. Had we—Jewish writers, teachers, and cultural producers—believed that we had achieved the best thing possible, we would have doubtlessly led our children in the same direction.

In Israel, this inner conflict has almost ended. Children there are raised in Hebrew. They're turned into Jews. It's true that, even there, people are not completely free of this conflict. Even there, the danger of assimilation always lurks. But there's a system there that works on its own. Kids go to school. They learn Hebrew, they study the Hebrew Bible, a few excerpts from the Mishnah, the Gemara, various books of interpretation. Their whole education, all of their dreams and ideals, are connected with Jews and Jewishness, though there have been attempts there too to turn kids into "Hebrews" rather than Jews.

We don't have this kind of system to help relieve this conflict. On the contrary, all outward forces work toward assimilation.

You sit among writers and, again and again, you hear the same complaint that Yiddish writers have no one to write for. There are no readers now and there won't be any in the future. Yiddish writers feel like they've gone bankrupt, though some try to delude themselves with optimism. Actors feel similarly. Parents who send their children to Yiddish school whine about the same thing. "So what if the kid knows a little Yiddish?" they ask. "What good will it do?" And if they aren't asking this question, then their in-laws are. The children are still young, but they also understand the situation. They know that very few people speak Yiddish. On the street people speak English. Movies are in English. For kids, Yiddish and Yiddishkayt are connected with their grandparents, with the old country, with Hitler's slaughters, and other such faraway or disturbing things. The kids themselves are experiencing an internal conflict.

What have our thinkers and spokespeople done to heal this conflict? The answer is—very little. We lack the spirit to delve deeply into these issues. We turn this question over and over, but we avoid putting it plainly. This is always the sign of an inner conflict. We're afraid to take our own pulse.

We talk about the practical side of elevating Yiddish culture. But there is no theoretician who can clarify to us why we actually need Yiddish culture at all. . . .

This writer often suspects that the majority of writers and cultural producers have quietly made peace with the thought that Yiddish culture is something personal to them—something of their time and place. Deep in their hearts they think, "We'll gather round each other and die out. Whatever comes next, we'll be gone." It's clear that with these kinds of thoughts and complexes, no important work can be created. . . .

Our religious grandparents had faith that God created the world, has providence over it, and chose the Jews as God's nation and gave them the Torah. The situation of the Jews has been sad ever since they transgressed and were driven out of the Land of Israel. But redemption awaits us. We will return to the Land of Israel. The dead will be resurrected. The greatest of good times are still *ahead* of us. Our grandfathers and grandmothers were great optimists. They built on a firm foundation.

What's left to us of this faith? Many modern Jews will tell you that there's nothing left. They don't believe in God or in the immortality of the soul, and they don't believe that Jews are different from German or Chinese people. One thing is certain: Jews are in trouble. But there are other peoples and groups who are suffering. In a better world, things would be better for Jews too. There's no guarantee that such a better world will ever come, but we have to strive for it simply because it's in our interest. It's strange, but there are many Yiddishists who think this way. In other words, the Yiddishists are those Jews who have the least amount of religious sentiment left in them.

When you ask such Jews, "In the name of *what*

should we preserve Yiddish language, Yiddish culture?" they're somehow always embarrassed. In Poland these Jews had an answer: the masses speak Yiddish, and since this is the language of the masses, we need to develop it and turn it into a better instrument. Here in America the masses no longer speak Yiddish, and this answer no longer exists. We can boldly say that, here, these Yiddishists have no answer. . . .

Let us state our opinion clearly: without faith in higher powers there is no foundation, neither for Zionism nor Yiddishism. Jews who believe that nothing is either kosher or unkosher, that Jesus is as good as Isaiah, and that Rabbi Levi Yitshak of Berdichev can be replaced by Saint Francis of Assisi—such Jews have no basis with which to cling to Yiddishkayt, not in Israel and certainly not in any other country. No matter what such Jews do for Jews or Jewishness, their deeds will remain under the sign of pure egoism. It will amount to nothing but a way of serving themselves, their ambitions, and their careers.

If above we talked about an inner conflict, it's only because the majority of Yiddish writers and activists are still far from convinced of their own materialist conception. In reality, the conflict revolves around the question of whether higher powers exist or whether the world is a machine.

Combining the preoccupation with faith found in both his first article on Holocaust survivors and the previous piece on the paradox of modern Jewishness, as well as his insistence that the problem of contemporary Yiddish literature is one of quality rather than quantity, Singer brings these conclusions to bear on the topic of reviving Yiddish language and culture in postwar America. Singer had raised the specter of the unconscious in his piece on modern Jewishness's inner conflict, referring specifically to Freudian theory, but here he proposes something that combines psychoanalysis and spiritual or religious thought: unconscious faith. He suggests that people who pursue activities with unknown outcomes—like those undertaking the unprecedented project of Jewish nation-building in the newly established State of Israel—must possess a measure of faith to which they don't refer in a spiritual manner. Singer makes a case for bringing out this unconscious faith and connecting it to the legacy of Jewish tradition in religious terms, though not necessarily in a way that would follow either Orthodox or Ultra-Orthodox precepts. He suggests that conscious faith, rooted in an awareness of Jewish tradition, might mitigate the inner conflict of modern Jewishness.

On the Revival of Yiddish Culture in America

(December 4, 1948)

We have shown that Yiddish culture cannot be built without faith in higher powers. Without any faith in the higher destiny of the Jewish people, there is no reason for Jews in America to want to bother themselves with Yiddish or Hebrew. Pure materialists have no reason to send their children to a school where they're taught Yiddishkayt. From a completely practical standpoint, Yiddish and Hebrew are in no way helpful for children—it doesn't strengthen their position in the struggle for existence. As we have shown, there is no materialist theory that justifies the struggle for Yiddish and Yiddishkayt in America.

Let us now make clear what we understand as our faith in higher powers.

There are two types of faith. One of them is a clearly defined faith like that of our grandparents. This faith was expressed in the so-called Thirteen Principles of Jewish Faith and in everything that Jews learned and did. It's the faith that the Jewish people maintained throughout two thousand years of exile.

Yet there's another type of faith—a faith that is not defined, not clear, but that ensues from our behavior, from our actions.

Halutzim who went to the Land of Israel to drain swamps, knowing that they were in danger of dying of malaria, were for the most part nonbelievers. They did not believe that the Torah was given on Mount Sinai. Many of them agreed with Bible critics. Some of them were even Marxists. But the very fact that these young people threw away their careers, took on all kinds of suffering, and risked their lives to build a Jewish country—this showed that deep in their hearts these people had faith. We don't sacrifice our lives simply for some theoretical notion. These young people's blood had absorbed the words of the prophets. The Land of Israel was not just a territory to them. It was a piece of something holy. This is a type of faith that lies hidden deep in the unconscious.

Just as there is unconscious doubt—unconscious desire, hate, envy, fear—there is also a faith that lies concealed deep in our psyche. We know of people who consider themselves to be freethinkers but who are nevertheless very superstitious. We know of avowed materialists who recite psalms in times of danger or promise to give charity. This writer believes that the majority of modern Jews are unconsciously religious. It literally pops out at you. Jews who supposedly believe in nothing build schools and studyhouses, send their kids to yeshiva, and do things that, from a purely logical standpoint, have no real justification. These Jews fasted during the time of Hitler's slaughters and cursed Hitler every chance they got with a death as horrible as that of Haman and every other Jew hater. Yiddish theater producers are familiar with this hidden Jewish religiosity. Nothing moves a Jewish audience more than the Hebrew words to the "Merciful God" prayer—*El Maleh Rahamim*. All of Yiddish literature is full of religious content. . . .

Unconscious religiosity and conscious unbelief represent the greatest internal conflict of modern Jews. All of our activities take place under the sign of this conflict. Generally, we could say that modern Jews have no desire to take on themselves the burdens of the Torah and the commandments. But they can't free themselves from the Jewish spirit. Somewhere inside we all believe in Judgment Day, in redemption, in the triumph of justice, in the special mission of the Jewish people. The Jewish state that has now been created has strengthened this faith. Somewhere inside we all see it as a miracle.

It is this writer's deepest conviction that a Yiddish culture that tries to deny our religiosity will never take hold. Such a culture has no rational foundation, nor can it stimulate any inspiration, not in parents and not in children. In a sense, Yiddish cultural producers today have to be like psychoanalysts. They have to conjure up the truth that lies buried in our souls. They have to lay down the foundation of their structure—not on the surface but deep down. They have to give us a culture that will match up with our demands and desires. If they don't, they will just run into a dead end.

It is no small thing to bring internal complexes out into the light. Modern Jewishness is as full of contradictions as pomegranates are filled with seeds. It is no easy thing at all to teach kids about the holiness of Shabbat at school, then their parents desecrate that same Shabbat. It's hard to get a child to understand the deep chasm that appears these days between our words and our actions. Often, modern Jewishness itself seems to be some sort of neurosis. But we know that nervousness can sometimes also be a source of creativity. Modern Jews have not been paralyzed by their internal conflicts. Despite all their doubts they have created a literature, resurrected a language, and fought for a country of their own. Modern Jewishness is currently an active volcano. We are witnessing new forms changing shape. We are fired up by energy rising from unreachable depths. We have no way of knowing when this new Jewishness will take on stable forms or what they will look like. But we are familiar with the energy that drives us. The fire that spoke from the mouths of our prophets has not been extinguished. It burns in us, it drives us, it evokes both hate and wonder from the world.

The fact that we want to build up Yiddish culture is quite clear to this writer. What's sad is that some of our builders want to deny this culture's driving force. They're afraid to look the facts in the face. They want to wrap the fire in the fluff of inane rationalizations. They want to distract not only everyone else, but themselves as well. . . .

It is not a lack of money that hinders the building up of Yiddish culture in America. It's a lack of spirit.

Yiddish culture in America—and in Israel as well—constitutes a major problem. We have to build within a tangle of conflicts. No matter what we do, we will never be able to satisfy everyone. There are fanatics among us who want to renounce Yiddish language and literature. There are those who try to belittle modern Hebrew and the Jewish state. There are those who demand that our culture be completely Orthodox. There are those who are still making use of the phrase "pure secularism." It isn't easy to bring unity to this chaos. But one thing is clear: Yiddish culture should be neither cold nor lukewarm, built on a theory that has long ago lost its logical and emotional foothold. And we'll say even more: The builders of Yiddish culture must have a youthful fire in them. It's better for it to be built by people with strong inner conflicts than by sleepy hair-splitters.

This writer is optimistic with regard to Yiddish culture in America. The same spiritual powers at work in Israel are quietly at work here. Time will bring forth new people and new opportunities.

In this article, Singer expands on his concern for the future of Yiddish literature, this time through his friendship with Aaron Zeitlin, the Yiddish poet, writer, and playwright he had met in Warsaw. Singer and Zeitlin had co-edited the literary journal *Globus*, in which Singer's first novel, *Satan in Goray*, appeared serially in 1933. Zeitlin had arrived in New York in August 1939 for the production of a play and remained there when World War II broke out, traveling to Cuba to receive his residency permit to stay in the United States. His wife, children, brother, and father were all killed in the Holocaust. Zeitlin returned to religious observance after the war, publishing a well-known poem, "I Believe" or "Ani ma'amin," in 1948. Singer's suggestion for a literary group that specifically mentions Zeitlin recalls their friendship in Warsaw, where they made plans to cowrite a trashy novel about Otto Weininger, a self-proclaimed philosopher and author of *Sex and Character* (1903). When Singer speaks of there being nowhere Yiddish writers can come together to meet and discuss literary or personal matters, he implicitly recalls the Association of Yiddish Writers and Journalists, of which both he and Zeitlin were members—and about which he eventually wrote many stories as well as a series of untranslated memoir-vignettes. This article might be seen as Singer's final attempt at a working plan to reestablish the infrastructure that had kept Yiddish literature alive in Warsaw and in his adopted home, New York City—less a manifesto than a road map for how to rebuild a living culture. In retrospect, none of these ideas was picked up by others in a way that reflected Singer's vision, and it seems he retained the core aspects that could be implemented on his own and integrated them into his literary vision.

A New Yiddish Literary Group?

(December 26, 1948)

It happens during people's lives that they fall into pettiness, or "small-mindedness," as the Hasidic rebbes called it. They lose perspective, forget their long-term goals, their faith in themselves and their duties. They get angry at every little thing. They get too involved in household issues. They listen to all kinds of gossip and walk around resenting everything. Such people become petty in their own eyes and in the eyes of those closest to them. In this writer's opinion, Yiddish literature has been in this kind of situation for a considerable period of time.

Yiddish literature, which began with great achievements—with major talent and big personalities—has given up, turned petty, and been unable to pick itself up. Books are published, but they somehow lack any flavor. Writers get into all kinds of petty arguments with each other. Their disagreements have no higher aims. There's a small clique that tries to promote itself at the expense of other writers. The pettier their spirits, the more they exaggerate the praise they heap on each other and on themselves. Literary criticism, which is supposed to be objective and, in a certain sense, to stand above writers, has itself fallen into this same unfortunate state. It chases its own tail. Rather than arousing courage, faith, or a will to be creative, it conducts petty politics, getting so tangled up in trivialities that it can no longer pull itself out.

Prizes are awarded, but a large portion of the books are not prize-worthy. Some of them should have been altogether torn to pieces. Others reek of mediocrity. Readers who are still interested in Yiddish literature see that people are dishonestly playing tricks on them, though they don't understand why.

There are people who were born petty but then underwent some sort of great tragedy. The kind of tragedy that was recently experienced by the Jewish people has, it would seem, never been experienced by any other nation. But even this tremendous blow has not awakened our Yiddish literature. Empty phrases have taken the upper hand. Prose writing, which was the foundation of our literature, is practically dead. A flood of poems has descended upon us, but most of them are so overworked, so insincere and boring, that they only elicit yawns. This writer sometimes gets the sense that the creative instincts have fallen into a stupor and that only one instinct remains awake: personal ambition. A large number of writers have found that they lack the moral strength to exist, so they latch on to politicians and political parties. This is their last place of refuge.

We cannot speak of the decline of Yiddish literature without mentioning external circumstances. Things are not going well for Yiddish. The older generation is dying out. The younger generation does not want to know *mame-loshn*. Assimilation in America is quite strong. These are undoubtedly oppressive conditions. But in these same tragic circumstances—even in circumstances that are much worse—Jews have resurrected a language, fought for their land, built communities, and blew the breath of life into a generation. Circumstances are not everything. Personality was created in a way that allows us to confront difficulties.

Let's take a moment to appraise our literature here in America.

There are five million Jews in America, five times more than in Israel. We are partially sustaining Jewish communities in Israel. We send hundreds of millions of dollars to our brethren across the entire world. Even the number of Yiddish-speaking Jews is still significantly high if we take into consideration the number of Yiddish newspapers that are published in America. We are a rich and robust community. We are generous with money. But in this great Jewish community there is not a single home for the intelligentsia. There is no physical place where intellectuals can get together. There is no institution here like the Yiddish writers' club in Warsaw. There is no library where a Yiddish writer or cultural producer can read the Yiddish press from all over the world or peruse a Yiddish book. The literary busybodies who spend so much time promoting themselves have maintained that such an address does not serve their petty interests.

There are a few publishers, but they too are controlled by a small clique. There is nowhere for Yiddish writers to publish their books. Those who do have access to a publisher are asked to publish the book at their own cost, and publishers actually offer nothing but a stamp of approval.

With no home and no publisher, Yiddish writers in America are more transient than any other community. You walk into the cafeteria on East Broadway on Fridays and see Yiddish writers pushing their way through crowds with trays in their hands. There's nowhere for them to sit, no way for them to talk properly about anything. There's no environment, no atmosphere, no body, no life.

Why are we exposing this bitter truth? Because this writer believes that it's not yet too late. It's never too late to repent. When dealing with spiritual questions, there's no such thing as too late.

If it wasn't too late to resurrect the Hebrew language or to settle Israel after thousands of years of destruction and oblivion, it's not too late to do something for Yiddish, the language that Jews have spoken for many hundreds of years and which was on the lips of our martyrs as they were killed. The Jewish people cannot be regenerated while Yiddish remains downtrodden.

What should we do in concrete terms? First, those writers who relate seriously to Yiddish and Yiddish-kayt—and not just to themselves and their reputations—should form a group. The members of this group should be writers as well as honest and genuine friends of Yiddish. The group should immediately find a home for Yiddish writers and a library for Yiddish literature. This home doesn't necessarily have to be magnificent. It doesn't have to become some big center right away. We have to begin somewhere. Yiddish writers have to meet face to face. The group has to make it clear from the outset that there's no room for the in-crowd at the helm. To the extent that we can, we have to free ourselves from the little dictators of our Yiddish cultural world. Little dictators have the same ethos as big dictators, and they do as much damage in their smaller environment as do the others in their own spheres. There were no literary cliques in Warsaw or Vilna, and there's no reason why they should dominate here in New York.

Second, we have to found a publishing company that will be owned by the writers themselves. If writers are able to publish themselves, they will not need to resort to cliques. The writers should put together an editorial team that will have the right to throw out a work that's bad and to revise the language of writers who make stylistic mistakes. With time, Yiddish organizations may help this publishing company.

Third, Yiddish writers must have the chance to read their manuscripts to their colleagues and to make use of their criticism before the book is published for general readers. Writers have to get used to getting critiqued by colleagues without turning them into enemies. We have to rebuild American Yiddish writers' relationships with themselves and with each other.

Fourth, Yiddish literature has to be in close contact with literature in Israel. We must, once and for all, stop inflating our ego and playing the role of the older sibling. It's a fact that our younger siblings in Israel are more inspired than we are, have more faith in Yiddish-kayt and a greater will to action. We have to draw from their source. We have to translate their work. We have to make a pilgrimage there and learn from their courage and devotion. Those who either openly or quietly belittle Israel and its spiritual achievements will never be spiritually redeemed. They will sink deeper and deeper into trivialities.

This writer is not naive enough to believe that all these suggestions can be carried out on the basis of a yes or a no. He's aware of the human constitution, as well as its psychological and physical situation. But he believes, at the same time, that it's not all over yet. The goodwill shown to Yiddish in Israel in recent times is proof that there too people appreciate the important role that this language has played in our fate.

This writer has discussed the idea of this group with his friend the Yiddish-Hebrew poet Aaron Zeitlin and has suggested calling it ALI, an acronym for *Am Levadad Yishkon* or "a nation that dwells alone." The idea is that those who belong to the group believe that the Jewish people was and must remain a discrete nation, with its own destiny, its own mission, its own worldview. He has expressed the correct opinion that the group should include both Yiddish and Hebrew writers since both languages express the Jewish spirit and character, each in its own way. The pettiness we spoke about is to a great degree also dominant among Hebrew writers. They too have little dictators with large appetites. They too have those who work according to the method of "scratch my back and I'll scratch yours," you call me a genius today, and I'll call you a genius tomorrow. Today you give me an award, and tomorrow you'll get one from me.

The in-crowd pretends to be highly optimistic. They blabber about confidence. In reality, they believe neither in Yiddishkayt nor in Yiddish literature nor even in any final judgment. They feel that in literature, as in the marketplace, you should do anything to make a deal. Deal-making and corruption are actually the traits against which the Jewish nation has been struggling since it has come into existence. What was Hitler if not a terrible dealmaker?

It sounds strange, but it's time for Yiddish literature to repent. We have to do some soul-searching and not be ashamed to confess our sins. We have to try and save what can still be saved. We must, despite our despair, do the work that has fallen to us. We have to purify the air or else be suffocated.

It's not easy to be a people that lives alone, and it's extremely hard to express the spirit of such a nation—its isolation, its fear, its hopes, its goals. It's a bitter task to be a Yiddish writer isolated among the isolated. But every tragedy is a challenge. We have not been put in this position to be petty, trivial, and trifling but to lift ourselves up and turn darkness into light.

Two years after proposing a Yiddish club and group—a call that largely
fell on deaf ears—Singer continued to plumb religious Jewish texts
and sources in his search for a path ahead for Yiddish literature.
Appearing after Singer's first epic novel, *The Family Moskat*, was
published in book form in both Yiddish and English, the piece may
express his frustration at the challenges of working between languages and cultures while trying to convey a complex lifestyle in
long-form literary fiction. Decades before a book like Philip Roth's
Portnoy's Complaint (1974) raised the debate of American-Jew-
ish literature that can be considered "good for the Jews" or "bad
for the Jews"—and years before Singer's own work was widely
translated into English and criticized for portraying Jewish sexu-
ality and immorality—this article points to what he perceived as
an overpropensity on the part of contemporary Jewish culture and
literature toward "looking good" and trying to adapt to mainstream
American society. It should be noted too that some of the material
edited out has to do with a critique of Sholem Asch, particularly
his turn toward Christian themes in Yiddish literature. Rather than
whitewashing Jewish history or culture, Singer calls for a literature
that can be honest with itself.

The Nature of Our Literature through the Ages

(November 26, 1950)

I leaf through our old Hebrew Bible and think, *Why did the Creator of the Universe give us such bad publicity?* The prophets presented us in a very bad light. Abraham let himself be persuaded by Sarah to send his son Ishmael out into the desert. Isaac loved his son Esau merely because he prepared him good food. Jacob tricked his father into giving him his blessing and then cheated Laban a little bit. Mother Rachel stole her father's household idols. Simon and Levi started a pogrom against the innocent people of Shechem. The tribes of Israel sold their younger brother as a slave. Even Moses, the greatest of the great, was not free of sin. After having two children with his first wife, Zipporah, he fell in love with an African woman and married her. King David sent the husband of a woman to war and then took the woman for himself. Their son, Absalom, slept with his father's ten concubines "before the eyes of all the Jews." His other son, Amnon, raped his half-sister Tamar. The Hebrew Bible even testifies that King Solomon worshiped idols.

The prophets call Jews by the worst names: thieves, robbers, murderers, adulterers. Jerusalem was compared to a prostitute. The Hebrew Bible is filled with dark prophecies about the nation of Israel—prophecies that have, unfortunately, been fulfilled. There's a sea of antisemitism in the Hebrew Bible, though there are many good words for Jews there too. Either way, these are the dire facts. Our prophets portray the Land of Israel as a place full of liars, swindlers, robbers, blood shedders. It seems that among all of the Jewish kings, there was only one, Josiah, who is said to have not done anything bad. All of the others worshiped idols.

This is the kind of testimonial we were given, our "certificate of pedigree," and we walk around with it proudly!

We say this in response to modern Jews who cannot bear to have even a tiny speck of dust flicked at our people. They demand only the "good," only "love." In Yiddish literature, they constantly hold up the example of Rabbi Levi Yitshak of Berdichev, who pleaded in favor of the Jews. Modern Jews want to be crowned and embellished in writing, they want to be defended against antisemites and to have countless good traits attributed to them. . . .

Today's Jews have adopted the policies of the non-Jews: You sling mud at your opponent. You and your own side have to be praised. Political parties follow the same path. The question of truth and lies plays absolutely no role. It's not only during election season that you're allowed to make up any malicious thing about your opponent—you can do it all year long. On the contrary, you have to surround your own people with honor and greatness, you have to absolve them of all their sins, you have to look away from all their crookedness. Because what's the use of fighting against your own interests?

It's obvious that in an epoch of such self-love and self-adoration, people expect the same thing from literature. If it can't serve one specific party, then it should at least serve them all. It should say only good things about our people, regularly seeking out what's "positive, healthy, vigorous." It should only focus on the good and the beautiful.

There is now a sort of campaign within Yiddish literature—and in Hebrew and anglophone Jewish literature as well—for positivism, and a war is being waged against those who refuse to sing with the choir. In Yiddish literature there has appeared a new religious floweriness. People pick out words and concepts from Hasidic and kabbalistic books, and they smear them all over long poems and treatises. Our books and newspapers are full of *dveykes* and *hisgales*, divine communion and revelation, full of Elijah the Prophet, the Messiah, Rabbi Yitskhak Levi, the Baal Shem Tov. Our literature has also begun dripping with dubious honey, with rancid sycophancy. Our people has turned ignorant. A number of writers have hitched themselves to all kinds of buggies. But what they write is so "lofty," so "divine," so nauseatingly sweet, that it makes you want to vomit. Obviously, our writing does not and cannot have any relationship to our life in America, which is ignorant, unlearned, materialistic, and assimilated. Jewish life goes in one direction and the writers go in their own. The parent writes about *dveykes* while the child often knows not a single word of Yiddish, not a single paragraph from the Hebrew Bible, and is not Jewish in any way. The parent—oozing *hisgales*, *dveykes*, and *kdushe*—never actually thinks about applying these good and noble traits to everyday life. Our literature is increasingly becoming a figment of our imagination.

You see the same thing in literary criticism. Writers have started glorifying each other with such words of praise that even complete idiots cannot take them seriously. Sometimes a single sentence contains so much light, radiance, greatness, and genius that it saves you from needing to read the next sentence. How much greatness can you pile into a single person? . . .

The Hebrew Bible is generally a bitter book, full of curses, angry prophecies, harsh words. It's notable that from today's assimilated perspective, even God is not shown in a very good light. The God of the Bible appears as an angry, jealous, vengeful God.

The Talmud and the religious authorities placed heavy burdens on Jews. They based everything on actions, not on words. Hasidic books were more moderate, but they too focused on actions and good traits. Hasidic books were written at a time when they reflected part of Jewish spiritual life. The Maskilim made many mistakes, but at least they wanted something concrete. They had an influence on Jewish life. They had harsh critiques. The same can be said about our classic Yiddish writers. One was more biting, the other made jokes, the third was a combination of the two. Our literature was, from the beginning, full of shadows. We never lit up every little corner.

For the first time in our history a Jewish literature has been produced out of "light" alone, only "goodness" and "holiness." Precisely now, when our life is so dark, so assimilated, so devalued and corrupted—precisely now our writers have decided to sing our praises twenty-four hours a day. They sing the praises of things that have nothing to do with our spiritual life, and they sing one another's praises too. Instead of combating this abnormal situation, our criticism encourages it. The criticism has itself discovered its musical tone. It has finally, finally lived to see the day for which it has always yearned: the eternal Shabbat when writers sit with their pens in hand, with the muses on their shoulder, milking an imaginary *Shekhinah*—a *Shekhinah* glued together with ink, paper, and lies.

This writer is far from being against a religious awakening. He is convinced that without religion the Jewish people cannot exist. But lying is not a religion. The Jewish religion has never been cut off from everyday life. It was always a lifestyle, something quotidian. It's clear that we cannot, at this time and in our current spiritual condition, go back to the countless rules and strictures that the rabbis placed upon us. This is why we have to return to the Hebrew Bible. But the falsified hymns that are sung on the Yiddish literary street, the empty rhetoric, the wild exaggerations, are all contrary to the spirit of the Hebrew Bible. We're not exaggerating in the least when we say that our smiley rhetoric comes from the unjewish world—where they preach love and practice hate, where from the beginning words hold no consistency or obligation, where lies are the foundation, where they demanded love and set out on inquisitions, where they spread the gospel of the Kingdom of Heaven and fought over every piece of the earth.

Both the body and the spirit of the Jewish people are covered with countless wounds. In the diaspora we're threatened with complete assimilation, and with partial assimilation in Israel. A new generation will grow up there that "did not know Joseph"—that does not want to know us at all. The party disputes there have reached such a state that anything is kosher in the name of the party and its interests. We've immediately gone down the paths there that have led to destruction. In a number of countries the Jews who remain are sinking into a kind of leftism that morally ruins them and physically grinds them down. Rather than courageously exposing our wounds, healing what can be healed and cutting away what needs to be cut away, we've embarked on a self-praising spree.

We can't take credit for the good deeds of the Baal Shem Tov. We barely have a relation to Rabbi Nahman of Bratslav. We are a generation of naked Jews. We have, with our own hands, led our children to complete ignorance and unjewishness. We ourselves are barely Jewish. Our lives are vulgar, loathsome. We're surrounded by enemies and we even hate ourselves. If we have respect for anything, it's everything that isn't Jewish.

Yet we don't have to fall into complete despair. This writer believes that the Jewish people will live on, though only God knows what will remain of us—and how many. What we need now are not superficial singers and croaking nightingales but people with spirit who have the courage to look truth in the eye.

If you look too long at the sun, you go blind. The only light that does no harm is the light of the truth.

In some ways, this article reflects a stage of Singer's thought during this period in which his call for a local club for Yiddish literature, in the style of the Association of Yiddish Writers and Journalists in Warsaw, is transformed into a description of shtetl life and the kind of Jewish culture that traditionally existed before Judaism came into direct conflict with modernity. As someone who grew up with the living culture of the Jewish studyhouse, and experienced its semi-secular version in the writers' club, Singer expresses the conviction that only a physical location where people can go to spend time and meet others can sustain Jewish life in the post-Holocaust period. Jewish institutions in the United States would only succeed in reinvigorating their culture, he argued, once they were made available to anyone and everyone who wanted access and sought interaction with others. In practice, as his memoirs and stories testify, the closest Singer ever arrived to re-creating this feeling outside of religious frameworks were the cafeterias he visited regularly, and about which he wrote in stories and memoirs much in the same way he wrote about the writers' club in Warsaw.

The Synagogue and the Studyhouse

(March 31, 1951)

We don't need to tell our readers about the difference between synagogues and studyhouses. They know
it all. Synagogues are usually impressive structures, but
rather cold. You never went to a synagogue to warm up.
It didn't even have a chimney. Synagogues never had any
books. They had only one purpose: prayer. The synagogue, as a house of prayer, is the closest thing we have
to a church. The studyhouse, as an institution, does not
exist in Christianity. It was a place where people prayed,
studied, smoked cigarettes, fried potatoes, talked about
business, politics, community issues. Poor Jews would
spend the night in the studyhouse. Slackers would stand
near the oven and tell stories. The studyhouse, the *besme-
dresh*, was actually a religious club.

For the most part, Jews who went to synagogue
were simple, unsociable, or *misnagdim* who opposed Hasidism—those for whom it was enough to get through the
prayer service and go home to their wife and kids. There
were also those who were busy and didn't have more than
the half an hour it took to get through the prayer service. The Jews who came to the studyhouse were those
for whom Yiddishkayt was everything: a religion, a way
of life, a form of entertainment, a social outlet, even their
business. They lived out their lives among the bare ta-
bles, oak podiums, and packed bookshelves. The younger

generation was literally raised there. Preachers would give their sermons there. This is where people yelled about the overly high tax on Passover flour that was set by the powerful. When there was a flood in the shtetl, and people who'd been displaced by floodwater needed to find an apartment, they were temporarily set up with bundles of straw in the studyhouse, where they slept. The studyhouse had a different sort of holiness from that of the synagogue: it was a human kind of holiness.

The synagogue was far from being a product of the diaspora. It existed in the most ancient times. The studyhouse developed mainly after the exile. The synagogue belonged to the Bible, the studyhouse to the Talmud and the Gemara. We don't exaggerate when we say that without the studyhouse, the Jewish people would not have endured two thousand years of bitter persecution.

Some time ago, this writer said that for Yiddish culture to live, it needs its own house, a home, a club. It's not for nothing that we wrote this. We relied on our two thousand years of experience. Not only all of Yiddishkayt but even half of Yiddishkayt can't exist without a home, a *shtibl* with books and a table, a place where people get together not by special invitation but freely, when they're in the mood and have some time. In Warsaw and Vilna, where Yiddish culture flourished for a while, there were many such places. . . . Every shtetl had a union, a library, often several unions or associations where young people got together, read, discussed, fantasized, hoped. The same young men would often also stop by the studyhouse to talk about something or even to dip into a religious book.

The Hasidic *shtibl* was in reality another kind of studyhouse. In the Hasidic *shtibls* you could do things that weren't always permitted at the studyhouse. Hasidim would drink a glass of brandy, sing, dance, joke around. They played chess and logic puzzles at the *shtibl*, and during Hanukkah they even played cards and spun dreidels. People did not only have the three traditional Shabbat meals at the *shtibl* but also a *melaveh malkah*, a festive meal held in the evening after Shabbat was over.

The New Testament makes a big fuss about people who changed money at the Second Temple. It makes it seem as if these moneychangers were hypocrites or outcasts. But it's a fact that during times of war, in these small shtetls, Jews changed money, engaged in the business of foreign currency, and it didn't make them any worse. Army recruits exchanged money for food in studyhouses and *shtibls* before reporting for duty. Jews didn't want to serve the tsar and they didn't want to lose their last groschen because of German or Polish decrees. The moneychangers from the Temple were far from the outcasts that the gospel and Sholem Asch make them out to be. Already then they looked at holy places as clubs for both human and divine matters. One of the characteristics of the Jewish religion is that it doesn't separate people from God.

One of the most characteristic aspects of the Jewish religion and of Jewish life is the small role played by bureaucrats. A rabbi had his table and chair, his few gilders per week, his courtroom, but he was never an intermediary between people and God. Very often the upper classes were more learned than he was. When it came to religion he was a Jew like anyone else. There were sometimes community leaders who abused their positions, but overall Jewish communities were handled in a thoroughly democratic manner. It's worth noting that the rabbi and the community leaders would generally go to services in the synagogue. There was no cantor in the studyhouse or *shtibl*. Anyone could go up to the lectern. There was no specific time for prayer services. When a quorum of ten Jews came together, they prayed. The students and young men who studied there did not "belong" to anything, they were not members of any organization. When a student wanted to study, he came into the studyhouse, took a book, and studied. When he wanted to go home, no one got in his way. The place was ruled by a kind of academic freedom that the most progressive scholars and professors dream about. The studyhouse was the deepest expression of the Jewish need for freedom.

It is this writer's conviction that until we bring the studyhouse back to life, Yiddishkayt will never be able to be resurrected, regardless of whether it is strictly religious Judaism or a Yiddishkayt that is mixed with secularism. No synagogue, organization, office, college, society, conference, congregation, or any other such institution can substitute this place where Jews could come any time they felt like taking a book, reading, discussing, and being in contact with other Jews. In the synagogue you finish praying and close the doors. In a large hall you hold a meeting and then turn off the lights. In institutions you hear a speech and then go home. None of these has the right atmosphere for the Jewish spirit. Jews don't want merely to listen to a lecturer. They want to articulate their thoughts too. They don't want anyone explaining spiritual issues to them with hard facts from the past. When it comes to anything having to do with Jews, they want to have an equal say. The greatest tragedy of American Jews is that they've been completely weaned off secular or religious books. Studying religion at home by yourself is not part of the Jewish tradition. Great scholars studied at home. Everyone else caught a bit of the Mishnah or some Gemara at the studyhouse. Even simple people would dip into a religious book and get something out of it. If people didn't know how to study, they listened as other people studied. They partook in debates and conversations. They told stories.

Yiddish culture—like modern culture in general—has turned simple people into silent witnesses. Lecturers lecture, scholars write books, poets compose poems, actors act in theaters, but simple people have only one role: to stay silent while watching or listening. Their role is completely passive. If they ever express their own thoughts, they send letters to the editor, but out of hundreds of letters only one is printed. Never has the public been as silent as it is today. . . .

Every living body is made up of cells. Jewish cells were made up of studyhouses and *shtibls*. Locked synagogues and public halls that are only opened for meetings, like organizations that put all their weight behind officials of every kind, cannot satisfy the spiritual hunger of our souls. They can continue existing and even growing, but as long as we don't have a studyhouse, the people will die of spiritual hunger. . . .

Singer repeatedly refers to the need to return to *sforim*, or religious books and commentaries, in his essays and articles from the 1940s—and here he delves into some of the ones that were being reprinted in the early 1950s. Lamenting the lack of interest in historical Jewish manuscripts when compared with those relating to English literature, he identifies works by Rabbi Menahem Meiri and the Seer of Lublin, two Jewish leaders who have since gained traction among religious scholars and thinkers. Singer focuses on modes and methods of penitence, another topic that he would explore and develop in his fiction for decades to come. He also admits that morality books are not often bestsellers in the modern world—and the fact that he could turn these topics into engaging and even award-winning literature in his lifetime points to his ability to transform religious material into literary fiction.

Old Religious Books Reprinted in America

(May 26, 1951)

Not long ago, Yale University published a manuscript called *London Journal 1762–63* by James Boswell, Samuel Johnson's well-known biographer. The manuscript was found in England and purchased together with other papers for tens of thousands of dollars. America and England are all up in a storm about this discovery from the eighteenth century. It would seem that a piece of old English culture has been reclaimed.

But was the world all up in a storm when Yeshiva University's Talpiot Publishing released Rabbi Menahem Meiri's *Hibur Ha'Teshuva*, a book of ethics and repentance? Yet this manuscript is a little older than Boswell's. It was stashed away for about seven hundred years. Now it has been printed with annotations by Rabbi Avraham Sofer of Jerusalem as well as an introduction and a biography by Rabbi Samuel K. Mirsky. Another person with a major role in reprinting this book is Reb Isaak Bulka of Nuremberg, who died in the Warsaw Ghetto. Reb Bulka sold religious books in Nuremberg. He had published an old manuscript, the *Mahzor Vitry*, a prayer book composed in 12th-century France. Hitler had already introduced the Nuremberg Laws, and yet in that same Nuremberg, Reb Isaak Bulka sat and copied out an old manuscript about what Jews should do as part of their penance. When the German Jews were sent off to ghettos and Reb Bulka ended up in Warsaw, he continued his sacred efforts. He obtained testimonials for the religious book from Reb Menachem Ziemba, Reb Chaim Ozer Grodzinski, and the Gerrer Rebbe. You would not know from these testimonials that Jews were dying of hunger and that all of European Jewry was being systematically wiped out. You'd think that the testimonials were written in the most peaceful of times. They show no sign of anxiety, fear, or weakness. The authors of these testimonials write that Meiri needs no testimonials, but that they still read through the proofs and that the book would certainly help Jews do penance. So people should buy the book and support the publisher.

The world makes a big deal about Boswell's *London Journal* and its brooding self-importance. This is "culture." But for Jews, a seven-hundred-year-old manuscript is hardly news. There are many manuscripts like this in the Vatican's library, at Oxford, in all kinds of archives. You can be sure this book will not be a bestseller. It would be a miracle if it sold a few hundred copies. . . .

I have another old book on my desk that is also an antiquity. It's the *Orhot Tsaddikim*, the *Ways of the Righteous*, a book of Jewish morality and ethics. The author did not indicate his name. We have no idea who he was or when he lived. It was surely hundreds of years ago. Why hadn't the author specified his name? Apparently because he didn't want the little bit of honor, or the great disgrace, that authors get for their books. Books were often published anonymously at that time. Why did the author matter anyway? The important part was the writing itself. *Orhot Tsaddikim* has been reprinted many times. It was studied in all the yeshivas that were occupied with ethics. It has now been reprinted by the Telshe Yeshiva in Cleveland, Ohio.

Another volume lies before me that recalls former times. This is the series called *Zot Zikaron*, *Zikaron Zot*, and *Divrei Emet*—*This Is Memory*, *The Memory of This*, and *Words of Truth*—by Rabbi Jacob Isaac Horowitz, the Seer of Lublin, as the Hasidim called him. It was published with the support of the Blum brothers, grandchildren of the Seer of Lublin, Rabbi Baer Radoshitzer, and the Ostrovtzer Rebbe. The introduction to *Zot Zikaron* is very characteristic of the Seer of Lublin. It's a kind of program on how to behave. It was probably written for his own use. In the past, many great figures wrote such notes for themselves. Here's a little bit of what the Seer of Lublin demanded of himself:

> Beware of pride and admit that you are worse than everyone else and all other living creatures. Beware of being angry, too, even at those who serve you, because they are better than you are. Beware of resentment, grief, flattery, lies, falsity, mockery of anything else (except for idolatry), ignoring religious study, and envy. Do not think about the material world at all or about any sort of pleasures. Your actions should be as hidden as possible. Think not about women and do not gloat when people yield to temptation, but, on the contrary, be sad for them. Be careful not to speak ill of others and do not talk about anyone in general, unless it is about those who are known for their righteousness (for when you speak well of an ordi-

nary person someone else might express a negative opinion). Don't suspect others and always give them the benefit of the doubt, pray for the public as well as for individuals, avoid disagreements even when they are about mitzvahs, don't cause anyone sorrow, don't shame anyone. Don't hold any victory over anyone's head unless it's for the sake of God. Hate no one. Do not take pleasure in honoring the Torah. Don't brag. Don't fear for your own honor but rather allow yourself to be scorned for the sake of God. Beware of melancholy. Don't consider what others think of you at all. Don't seek power.

And on and on—the notes continue for almost two pages in small type. This is what the Jews of olden times demanded of themselves!

It's interesting to note how the *Orhot Tsaddikim* conveyed different forms of penance. People who stole something or took interest on a loan had to ask the person who was wronged for forgiveness and fast for forty days. People who had taken interest on a loan should never lend money again, not even to non-Jews. People who inform on their friends should pay damages for everything and ask for forgiveness. Then they should be lashed and fast every day for more than two years. Gossipers should ask their victims for forgiveness, fast for forty days or more, and be lashed every day for the rest of their lives. People who shame friends should fast for forty days or more, ask them for forgiveness, and confess to the end. A man who has lived with another man's wife should, during winter, sit in snow and ice between one and three times a day. During the summer he should sit among flies or bees and confess with sighing and weeping. He should not eat bread or wash himself for an entire year, just a little before Shabbat and holidays. He should hear no laughter nor allow himself any pleasures, should be lashed every day, and should sleep on the bare ground or on a board without pillows and without any blanket. Only on Shabbat and on holidays may he lie down on straw.

Such words arouse laughter from people today. But these Jews were completely serious. Had Boswell read *Orhot Tsaddikim* with some attention, his *London Journal* would have likely looked very different, and it wouldn't have been a bestseller either. . . .

In this article, Singer articulates another point in his ongoing assessment of the problem of modern Jewishness, specifically identifying the lack of personal philosophy or worldview as one of its core issues. Whereas before he had focused on the question of faith, pointing either to its absence or its being relegated to the unconscious, he shifts here to the articulation of a worldview or attitude toward the world—something to which he returns in the last piece in this collection. His critique of secularism, socialism, and Zionism is that they are all ideologies without a perspective on personal life, on the way individuals should live and relate to each other, on the morals and principles that strengthen a group's social fabric. In response to this spiritual crisis or catastrophe, as Singer calls it, he points to the need for a code of conduct to spiritually guide the personal and communal lives of Jews in the modern world.

What Is the Foundation of Jewish Culture?

(September 15, 1951)

If we wanted to speak about the tragedy of modern Jews, we might say that it consists in their not having produced any philosophy of life and a lifestyle that goes with it. Modern Jews excel in many fields, including philosophy, but they have not produced their own worldview. Zionism is a political ideology but not a worldview that leads to a particular lifestyle. We can speak of the philosophy of ancient Judaism. But contemporary Jewry has not found it necessary to spiritually ground its own existence.

A very large number of modern Jews say they just happen to be Jewish. Reform Jews go to synagogue to show that they are not radicals. Modern Jews often have the sense that being Jewish obliges them to nothing. They're free. You might say that they live in a spiritual vacuum. Right before our eyes we see millions of Jews who themselves received Jewish educations and who are now raising their children without any Jewish knowledge. These Jews have harsh criticism for the old way of life—for the heder, the mikveh, the poorhouse. But they have not tried to find a new Jewish path or a new Jewish way of thought. Even in Israel, or rather *precisely* there, the lack of a higher ideology is visible. Many Hebrew writers complain that young people are materialistic, vacuous, indifferent to ethical values and to our spiritual heritage.

The Jewish emancipation happened to have come

together with the rise of materialism across the world. Modern Jews left the *Shulhan Arukh*, which controlled their every step, for a life where people did whatever they wanted, or as it was put in the Book of Judges, "They each did what was right in their own eyes"—everyone did whatever they liked.

This did not take such extreme forms among our neighbors. First, each country still had its own aristocracy, with its formality and rules. Second, there was also a large peasantry who had its own traditions. Third, the bourgeoisie remained more or less religious, as much as it could be called that. Fourth, there were institutions like the army, the navy, and all kinds of established organizations, each with its own rules of conduct, its own strong relationship to the nation's history and roots.

In our case, those who left the studyhouse were left without any spiritual guidance. They often became nihilists. Then came mass migration. Jews emigrated and exchanged their clothes, language, and customs. A great confusion overtook our lives and made them formless.

As mentioned, Zionism never transcended the framework of a thoroughly political movement. Jewish radicalism did partially influence private Jewish life, but it made a great many mistakes. The greatest among them were its destructive relationship to religion, at least in its early years, as well as its strong opposition to Zionism. Then came Communism, which took hold of many of our intellectuals and masses. Communism found it necessary to vilify everything that had to do with old Yiddishkayt, but it never produced even the shadow of a positive Jewish ideology. All it did was to waver between assimilation, settling the Jewish Autonomous Region of Birobidzhan in Siberia, and some provisional form of Yiddishism.

A people who had, for two thousand years, been instructed on how to eat and speak was left literally without any direction for how to live. For others, Jews became materialistic little money-grubbers who stopped at nothing when competing with them in business. If they were rich they were snobs. If they were poor they were revolutionaries. And if they tried to mix with locals they were fakers and saboteurs. Modern antisemitism didn't have to invent blood libels. It simply took our real faults and magnified them. You often hear Jews make the same complaints about other Jews that antisemites make about them. This is all because we've left behind a tremendous life of discipline for a life without any kind of spiritual responsibility. If we still have a lot of ethical people among us, it only proves that a century and a half cannot destroy what two thousand years have built up.

Many people in Israel are now very concerned about this precise spiritual barrenness. It is quite apparent there because it is a Jewish country where people live close to each other, where it's crowded, where the conditions are poor, and where every defect, bad reasoning, and false theory comes to light. In other countries Jews can afford to look away, to make themselves forget. But our enemies never forget. They're delighted by our faults. Esau was quite satisfied that Jacob—whose name became Israel—was left spiritually rattled, insecure about his behavior, and inclined to imitate his own worst adherents.

This is where we come to the question of culture.

When we build a Yiddish theater and put on Broadway-like productions, when we produce a literature that follows the ways of a Hemingway or a Yesenin, or when our ambition is all about proving that we *too* can take part in the drama of the general culture and sing along with the large choir—when we do this, we place ourselves even lower than grass. It is very tragic that a people who, for thousands of years, has struggled for its own philosophy, for its own spiritual world, should turn into a supporting actor or backup singer in its old age. The average Jew asks: "If I'm already imitating non-Jews, why not imitate them fully?" The tragedy of those who have tried to produce a modern Jewish culture is that they haven't posed the most important question: How are we supposed to compete with the others? What will make our culture better, more attractive, loftier? What can we actually give those who want to join our ranks? What can this culture actually give *us*?

Modern Yiddish and Hebrew culture has chiefly limited itself to language. In fact it is a culture that has been translated, even though this or that work may be original.

The truth is that Jewish culture, like Judaism generally, has to stand on the same foundation on which Judaism has stood all these years: faith in God and in God's providence and on our obligations to the higher powers. Without God Jews are simply negative people. They are *not* not Jewish. This is true even in Israel. The Hebrew language and the little hope that this small and poor country offers are not enough to maintain such an ambitious and life-loving nation like the Jews. . . .

If we wanted to convene a conference on Jewish culture today, we'd have to start over again. Certainly Yiddish and Hebrew are our languages, and everything we produce should be done in our own tongue, not in anyone else's. But the main question is: How can we get rid of the curse of being adherents or epigones and go back to being original? How can we produce a culture that will have an effect on people and their lives? How can we cover up our nakedness? How can we give form and content back to masses of people who are morally distressed and crestfallen—uprooted from our origins and not even connected to those we try to imitate? The question of Jewish culture is directly tied to a reappraisal of our religious values. Before we start producing culture we have to know what we believe in, what we take on as duties, and what is forbidden to us. Moral chaos can lead only to imitation, never to a dignified path.

We sum up our article with the following words: There can be no Jewish culture if modern Jews don't produce some sort of credo for themselves—some sort of *Shulhan Arukh*, some discipline. People who want to belong to a group have to be obligated by something moral. Language alone is not enough. It is surely not enough for a people with such a vast spiritual heritage as the Jewish people.

If millions of Jews in a single generation, in a single country, fail to give their children a Jewish education, we are dealing with a spiritual catastrophe. Not only are our calculations wrong, but our axioms—our fundamental principles—are mistaken. If we want to exist, we need to start over at the beginning.

What we've said about Jewish culture is actually true about modern culture as a whole. Spiritual people of all nations are terrified by the vacuity that surrounds all of modern culture as well as its institutions. For them, everything is actually about money. For them, culture is a commodity that can be sold on the marketplace. We don't even have a market, which makes our vacuity that much more tragic.

In the previous article, published only two weeks earlier, Singer declared, "If we want to exist, we need to start over at the beginning." He seems to answer his own call and undertake the project himself, beginning with the core concepts of good and evil. Though he had written about these topics before, he now sets off on a new way of approaching the issue, pointing specifically to the kinds of concepts that were used and that framed thinking in the past. He shows how, just a few generations earlier, the concepts of good and evil were clear to people—while anchoring them to the figures of the wicked and righteous, an approach that emphasizes the element of free choice. This is one of the early instances where Singer begins to integrate his own worldview, in which the human spirit is harnessed through free choice to lift behavior above base human nature. Though he would only articulate these connections directly decades later, we see him beginning to work toward meeting the standards he himself set for mitigating and breaking through the internal conflicts and paradoxes of modern Jewishness.

Righteous and Wicked—Words We No Longer Use

(September 29, 1951)

There are some concepts that modern society believes to be thoroughly unscientific and vague. Among them are the concepts of *righteous* and *wicked*.

For our grandparents these concepts were both clear and concrete. Haman was wicked and Mordecai was righteous. Informers in the shtetl were wicked, and Jews who prayed, studied, fasted, were honest, and gave charity were considered righteous. These two concepts were as clear for the older generations as day and night, summer and winter, the heavens and the earth.

Then came a sort of spiritual attack that was supposed to nearly erase these two words from the dictionary and relegate them to the archive where old words and concepts lie and rot, dead and forgotten. First, people showed that *wicked* and *righteous* were relative concepts. Someone who is righteous in one country is wicked in another. What was considered holy at one time was considered impure in other epochs. This meant that *wicked* and *righteous* depended completely on circumstances and had no absolute value. Additionally, these concepts were above all antiscientific. In every creature's struggle for existence, there's no room for such designations. Can we call the wolf wicked and the sheep righteous? And aren't humans subject to the same biological laws as animals? Isn't all of human progress the result of bitter struggles for life and death? Then who are the righteous and who the wicked? What value do the concepts of good and evil hold in the jungle? Modern thinkers altogether stopped using these concepts except in quotation marks, with a wink, a smirk, and a glance backward toward the unscientific past.

Freeing us from these concepts was not easy, and people had to come up with many, many substitutes. They started using words like *progressive* and *reactionary*, *positive* and *negative*, *yea-saying* and *nay-saying*, *useful* and *harmful*, *creative* and *destructive*, and many other such types of words, all of which were supposed to express the elementary concepts of good and bad in a way that's more appropriate for current times and circumstances. In Soviet Russia you no longer say that people are wicked. Instead you call them Trotskyists, saboteurs, fascists—all words that arouse horror the way the word *wicked* did in the past. In democratic countries too there are plenty of words to express that certain people are self-serving, harmful, destructive, corrupt. One word that's quite close to the concept of *wicked* is *outcast*.

But there's one big difference between the old concepts and the new ones that have replaced them. The words *righteous* and *wicked*—*tsadik* and *roshe*—were very clearly defined for Jews, very precisely delineated and determined. But the modern words that have replaced them are vague. During elections one group calls the other by all kinds of bad names that no one takes too seriously, neither those that do the name-calling nor those called by such names. The same is true of words of praise. You may read that people are noble, positive, useful, creative—then writers turn things around with a "but," and it turns out that they're bothersome fools, losers, or swindlers. The thousands of words that have replaced *righteous* and *wicked* somehow have no substance— they're far more relative, far more vague and blurred. When you called someone a *tsadik*, you could not add a "but." But words today, both good and bad, have lost almost all meaning. First people praise someone to the skies, and then they sling mud at them. Very often this is done together by the same writer using the same pen. Words no longer count for anything. Opinions have become so loose, so slippery, no serious person can make heads nor tails of them. You can read that someone is a pariah and realize that they are a highly moral person. You hear a thousand good things about certain people and then discover someone petty or a complete scoundrel. The gold coins of *righteous* and *wicked* have been exchanged for a bunch of inflation-ridden banknotes with big numbers and little value, or ones that are altogether worthless. . . .

If this were merely about a confusion of words, it wouldn't have been such a tragedy. In reality, it's about a confusion of concepts, judgments, values. It's not only in literary journals and political brochures that words are being violated and people are being judged without ceremony. The confusion has entered the hearts and minds of middle class people too. Even your average person on the street has learned to speak in two voices at once, saying "yes" and "no" about the same thing. People today are completely confused by all of these babelized phrases, hearing all of these ambiguities and equivocations. The general public has learned to spin things as well as any shystery lawyer or shameless politician. Yes and no, big and small, brilliant and boring—they've all become strangely similar. All this word- confusion comes together with a kind of moral chaos.

Isn't it time to take another look at the old concepts of *righteous* and *wicked*? Are they really so outdated and stale as people would like us to believe?

The truth is that without these words the human species cannot exist. It's true that these words were interpreted differently by different religions. But it's also true that, in moral terms, all major religions had roughly the same ideas about good and evil. Rabbi Levi Yitshak of Berdichev would have been considered a *tsadik* by Christians, Muslims, and Hindus. Gandhi would have been seen a *tsadik* by Jews as much as he is by Hindus. When it comes to moral values, all religions clearly delineate what is good and what is evil. They all accord with the framework of the Hebrew Bible's classifications. All religions and all classical ethical thinkers of all kinds would sign their names to the chapter of Psalms that says,

> God, who will live in your tent? Who will dwell on your holy mount? Those who walk upright, do justice, and speak truth in their hearts. They do not use their tongues for slander, they do no evil to friends, and they do not insult those closest to them. They despise the disgraceful and honor those who fear God. They keep their promises even when it hurts them. They do not lend money for profit and do not take bribes against the innocent.

These words are clear and even scientific. They classify good and bad as precisely as possible. No "but" can follow them to turn them on their heads. Many generations lived with these concepts. Many great people learned from them.

The jargon used by today's so-called intellectuals is often a mask that covers up a lack of spirit and a kind of cannibalism—a way of coping with criticism. Equivocation has always been and is still today a symptom of the wicked. Here they praise someone and there they insult them. Here they lift them up and there they knock them down. What's kosher today is unkosher tomorrow and what's unkosher today is *glatt* kosher the next day. The same confusion is taking place in courts of justice. There too the question of who's a criminal and what's a crime becomes less and less clear. The rules and principles there have become very loose and slippery.

Words themselves are not a sickness but a symptom. Behind words lie actions. In our current times, when words play such a colossal role, when the world is literally filled with typewriters and printers, when billions of words are disseminated daily at the speed of light, the tragedy of words cannot be waved aside. The world cannot be redeemed as long as words remain a tool of the wicked. . . .

Developing the idea of starting over, Singer reviews another aspect of
    Jewish life and culture that he considers fundamental: the rule of
    law. This connects to his personal concept of religion, which in-
    cludes rules demanded from us through our connection to higher
    powers. Having a spiritual feeling was never enough for Singer. He
    always insisted that faith brings duties or obligations—though for
    him the rabbinical form of these "mitzvahs" was outmoded. The
    question of what can replace Orthodox or Ultra-Orthodox practice
    is never fully treated in Singer's writing, where he urges individuals
    to develop their own religious conceptions and duties. Still, this ar-
    ticle gets close to articulating the need for an inter-group consen-
    sus about what it means to be Jewish after the Holocaust.

Jews and the Rule of Law
(May 31, 1952)

How is it that large businesses making millions go under?
How do powerful empires fall? A deeper look at history
and at human pursuits shows that the causes are always
spiritual. Rome did not *need* to fall. It collapsed because it
had accumulated so much evil and even more dishonor.
The will of its leaders was weakened. They continually
appeased the barbarians. They oppressed their friends,
indulged their enemies, sabotaged their own interests.
Before the physical breakdown, there was a spiritual
breakdown. In our time, Russia and Austria fell in similar ways. If empires had the time and will to learn from
experience, they would know that an ounce of dignity
and honor is worth more than tons of gunpowder. People who are worn out, who have no willpower, no back-
bone, no moral principles—such people live comfortably
enough on their own. But when many such people are
accumulated, it leads to collapse.

When a business collapses, the private firm or company declares bankruptcy. When countries are bankrupt,
dictators appear. Dictators are not the beginning of a
sickness but its end result. You can sense the overall dis-
content long before the dictators show up. The leaders
sabotage one another. The people suffer spiritually more
than they do physically. You get used to the idea that
there are no real laws, that everything is built on nepo-

tism, who you know, monkey business. In the depths of their hearts, people strive for lawfulness, not for chaos. When things are based on sycophancy and intrigues, on coincidence or on injustice, when they're full of absurd whims and surprises, they soon fall apart, even if the nation is militarily strong.

The cause of every revolution—in a nation, in a family, in a business—is lawlessness. As long as there is rule of law, some set of principles—even if it's strict—people can bear them. As long as people know what's allowed and what's prohibited, how they get into trouble and how they avoid it, they can somehow get along within the system. When they're convinced that their lives and activities are like a lottery, a game governed by random and uncontrollable forces, they start to get furious.

This is not a general sociological article but rather one that will explain the history of the Jewish world and our current situation.

Judaism was from the very beginning built on law. The Torah has for four thousand years been the constitution of the Jews. This constitution has had many amendments. Quite often, so many laws were invented—such harsh laws—that the burden became immense. But Jews were obedient. Despite all of the strictness and all of the burdens, Jews knew exactly when they sinned and when they did good. They had a clear concept of what was demanded of them, and they made an effort, according to their strength and willpower, to remain within the framework of the law.

Old-time Jews came into contact with the non-Jewish world and discovered that it was ruled by lawlessness.

According to Jewish concepts, wars were waged without rhyme or reason. They glorified people who did not genuinely deserve it. They persecuted people who hadn't sinned. The non-Jewish world of ancient times and especially the early Middle Ages—with its strongmen, with its open and hidden idol worship, with its false judges, corrupt police, mercenary armies, half-crazy knights—was for Jews what was called *mishpatim bal yeda'um*—laws that could not be properly learned because there is nothing proper to learn. It was a world ruled by whims and lawlessness, and when Jews returned to the ghetto in the evening, they breathed a sigh of relief. Here, between these narrow walls, there were clear laws and a precise pattern for life. Here they had precisely defined concepts of good and evil, what's beautiful and what's ugly. Spiritual life here was not lawless.

In modern times, Jews began to see that things were clearing up on the other side of the ghetto. More or less proper laws were being passed. People there diligently studied the laws of nature, and the situation had changed so much that the physical and spiritual world outside the ghetto was more lawful than life inside. Those who were strictly religious continued to claim that these were still the same *mishpatim bal yeda'um*, but the Haskalah captured a greater and greater part of the Jewish world. In the ghetto they created ever stricter laws. On the other side, a rich jurisprudence had been created, international law, and an extensive natural science. Jews, with their feeling for study and intellectual discipline, could not remain indifferent. They were carried away.

Then came the disappointment. Jews discovered

that, it was true, as far as natural science was concerned, a lot had been achieved in the non-Jewish world. But the laws meant to regulate life were superficial. Beneath them flowed the same old lawlessness. The nation was supposedly for everyone, but everywhere, at every step, there were privileges. You were grabbed, assaulted, beaten, and robbed no less than in older times. The justice system was no justice system at all, and laws weren't laws. Going back to the ghetto was difficult, and Jews decided to do what they could to bring rule of law into the non-Jewish world. Jewish liberalism emerged, striving for genuine rather than false equality. It tore off the masks. It showed how laws were violated. In every parliament, Jews thundered against power politics, nepotism, the plundering of the masses, and ethical lawlessness. The non-Jewish world responded with colossal hatred. This was no longer the hate of fanatic priests or jealous shopkeepers but a hate for those who were given equal rights and who, instead of being grateful, criticized, rebuked, or tore everything up into pieces. A slogan emerged among non-Jews which basically meant either go back to the ghetto or be completely annihilated. The Jewish ghettos of Hitler's Europe were a direct outcome of this very drama.

Many Jews saw that waging war against the world for the sake of integrity and rule of law was not within the powers of their people and argued that, if we want integrity and lawfulness, we need to build our own country. In a country of our own we'll be able to apply a true, untainted, unmasked rule of law. Jews, Torah, and the Land of Israel are united. *Ki mitsiyon tetse Torah*—the teaching and the law will issue from Zion.

Looking at the Jewish people as a people who has survived thanks to its inner lawfulness and thanks to ideals that are linked to the rule of law helps us understand many of the events that have taken place in Jewish history. It also helps us comprehend the suffering of Jews today.

Jews have suffered many disappointments in the world. Non-Jews assumed that Soviet Russia was the work of Jews. It was created by Jews. But even if this were true, it would be Jews who would be left most disappointed by "their" work. Soviet Russia has turned out to be a country ruled by whim—the power of a dictator. You never know, there, whether what you're doing is good or bad. The righteous today are the wicked tomorrow. A book that's praised today is tomorrow's heresy. You can literally say that this country is ruled by *mishpatim bal yeda'um*, laws that can't be learned or figured out. Laws are actually improvised by the minute, according to the leader's mood. There is nothing consistent, nothing solid. The dialectic is actually the total opposite of the law. It turns the law into a liquid substance that's so fluid you can do with it what you want and whatever serves you best. This is also why it's no wonder that Jews there have had to bear so much suffering to this day. Jews cannot exist, neither physically nor spiritually, in a lawless environment.

It is not necessary to describe the lawlessness of fascism. There, lawlessness reached such diabolical heights that it had to be quickly liquidated. Life itself had simply become impossible. There were less laws there than in the jungle, less laws than in a madhouse.

The free world should be—and in reality is—the Jews' only comfort and hope. But it too is to a great degree filled with disappointments. For a people that has sanctified the law, the laws of the non-Jewish world are too soft and lenient to satisfy the Jewish spirit. We aren't speaking here of jurisprudence in particular but rather of all of the rules of life, the written and the unwritten. Today's Jews may be spiritually very far from the ghetto and its strict observance, but it's hard for them to tolerate the outside world—its secularism, let's call it, with its leniency, its loose relationship to people, to words, to moral values, to the concept of justice. Is this what it was all about? Is this the "outside world," the enlightened world that the Haskalah praised to the skies? There is too much depravity there for the truly Jewish spirit, too much politics, too much indifference toward higher values. Not only here but even in Israel, in their own country, Jews often fail to find a deep connection to the law that they suckled with their mother's milk. . . .

In such a situation, it's no wonder that there are those among us who are returning to religion. There are Jews who feel that in the *Shulhan Arukh* at least they can find firm laws, a clear and single-minded way of life. But can Jews today go back to the *Shulhan Arukh* without any second thoughts?

A great spiritual conflict is taking place among modern Jews. We are now, as we were when we left Egypt, a thoroughly tormented nation, with great vitality and with a need for a spiritual leader as well as a system of laws. Just as four thousand years ago, Jews today cannot live without the law, without a clearly defined way of life.

We continue to suffer from *mishpatim bal yeda'um* that have surrounded us and that have invaded our own ranks.

As long as there is no Jewish legislation that says precisely what Jews are, and what is expected of them, Jews will remain a confused and disoriented people, wanderers in a world of chaos. Mount Sinai calls to us as it did four thousand years ago: "Accept the law—or be buried right here!"

A month after his article on the rule of law, Singer continues developing his reflection on what it means to be Jewish in the post-Holocaust era, this time connecting Jewish culture's need for legal structure to what he sees as the model for free societies after World War II: the American Constitution. Singer proposes using the American Constitution—which, he argues, shares the ideal of justice with the Torah—as the basis of a Jewish Constitution that would express the values that make Jews a distinct group. He acknowledges that there is never an ideal that is perfectly or fully realized, notes that ideals are meant to point toward a direction or path, and suggests that what Jewish idealism adds to the American ideal of justice is its faith in the power of the spirit over the material world.

Americanism and Jewishness

(June 28, 1952)

It would seem that in no other country do people discuss
the issue of nationality as much as they do in the United
States. Americanism is an eternal topic: Who is a real
American? What is Americanism? Rarely do people in
France or England discuss what it means to be French
or English. This is because America is a country made
up mainly of immigrants, and most of its people either
immigrated themselves or descend from quite recent immigrants. It lacks those national symbols and historical
hallmarks that the citizens of ancient and homogeneous
nations carry with them. America is still a mishmash of
different nations. No matter how much the melting pot
melts, it has not yet melted America's human material together. There are all sorts of mixes of races and nation-
alities. In the big cities there are neighborhoods where
immigrants lead their separate lives and speak their old
languages. It isn't easy to take people who are Black, In-
dian, Chinese, from New England, Jewish with sidelocks,
Japanese, Filipino, German, Russian, Polish, and Spanish and label them all "American." The same question
keeps coming back: What does it mean to be American?
What kind of a people are *Americans*?

In America, people have increasingly come to the
conclusion that Americanism is built mainly on accepting certain principles, laws, ideas. Americanism is built

mainly on the worldview that's articulated in the Constitution, on its rights and privileges, the principles and
ideals of America's citizenry. It's true that, technically
speaking, an American is anyone with citizenship, anyone who is born in the country. But in a deeper sense
Americanism is built on ideals. People who are propo-
nents of dictatorship are only technically Americans.
They're not American in their blood and soul.

This is where the remarkable similarity between
Americans and Jews really stands out. It's true that Jews
have their lineage, but after two thousand years of exile
the Jewish race has been left far less pure than it was
in earlier times. Our blood is mixed, as we see from the
many Jews who are blond. In the countries where they
live, Jews not only take on the clothing and customs of
the locals but also their appearance. . . . No, our racial
lineage is not enough to hold Jews together. Obviously,
until now, we also didn't have a shared country, economy,
or political system. What actually kept Jews together was
their faith, which is also an ideal. As much as Americans
discuss the topic of who is American, we do even more
discussing of who is Jewish.

When the Haskalah began dominating the Jewish
street and millions of Jews lost their faith, the question
of Jewishness became oddly acute. The whole issue of
Jewishness turned into an unsolvable riddle, like fitting
a square peg into a round hole. What connects a revolutionary Jew from Russia to a religious Jew from Yemen?
What connects a Jewish scholar from Berlin to a Jew
from Bukhara? What makes a Jewish American vaude-
ville actor and a Jewish Hungarian circus-horse rider like

brothers? What connected Warsaw's Professor Samuel Dickstein with New York's Jacob Schiff with a Jew who had a harem in Constantinople? The differences in all these places grew so large that the only distinguishing feature of a Jew lies in their being hated by antisemites. The mark of a Jew became altogether negative. It came not from within but from without.

Setting aside the Jews who now live in Israel, the question still stands for all the other Jews in the world: What binds them together? And no matter how much we argue the point, we have to come to the conclusion that the bond is ideological. There has to be some ideal that binds all these people who speak different languages, live in different countries, follow different customs. Lineage alone and hate alone cannot keep them together. And, anyway, hate needs something to stick onto.

German rabbis have used oceans of ink to express what comprises Jewish unity. A great part of the Jewish left has altogether denied the idea of Jewish peoplehood. A series of extreme Zionists have predicted that without our own country we'll be completely ruined. In different ways, Hitlerism on the one hand and the rise of Israel on the other have strengthened Jewish interest in far-off brothers and sisters. But these are temporary injections, not complete cures. Just as they were twenty years ago, Jews today still represent a bitter problem in the different countries where they live. The destruction of the deeply faithful and thoroughly singular Jews of Eastern Europe has aggravated the situation. We are in danger of becoming a nation that's torn to pieces. Israel will lead to the development of a Hebrew-speaking Jewry. In other countries Jews will be so deeply assimilated that they will ultimately mix with local populations. With our own eyes we've seen Russian Jewry be watered down and practically wiped out. In America they raise Jews who know nothing. Jews in Europe consist of scraps and remnants. And there are pessimists who say that when World War III breaks out and Jews in Israel suffer, God forbid, heavy losses, then it's too late.

As strange as it sounds, Jews today need a constitution—a clear and simple designation of Jewish values and obligations.

Strictly Orthodox Jews say that there's already such a constitution: the Torah, the Talmud, and the religious commentaries. Historically, this is true. But the existence of a maximalist constitution does not preclude the possibility of a minimalist constitution. Jews today have to identify those values on which everyone—or almost everyone—can agree, and these values have to represent the most basic form of Jewishness. In other words, we have to be clear on those values that, if rejected, make us no longer Jews in the ideal sense of the word, just as Americans actually stop being American if they try to eliminate the American Constitution and the Bill of Rights. . . .

The American Constitution was far from being built on a scientific foundation. It does not express matters of action but rather the ideal of justice. The notion that all people are created equal and have equal rights in no way agrees with history or even with biology. Some of the clauses in the Constitution are flexible. The American people can make amendments and even abolish certain clauses. The soul of the American Constitution is the *ideal* of justice—an ideal that points toward a direction but can never be fully achieved. This same ideal is actually the essence of the Hebrew Bible. The American Constitution itself represents a small bit of Jewishness. This writer believes that the American Constitution—which can and should become the constitution of the world—should be amended by modern Jews with their own unique ideals, those values that distinguish Jews from their neighbors.

In this writer's modest opinion, the following clauses should be among those considered:

1. Faith in Jewish peoplehood, the existence of which some have tried to deny in our time. This is a faith that a people is a people only when no external circumstances—no human or natural acts of violence—can tear it apart. Neither enemies, time, place, language, oceans, nor dictators can tear apart the bonds of their souls. Such a bond has existed among Jews for four thousand years and can exist forever. Jewish continuity consists of a fellowship that no physical force can abolish.

2. A faith that this Jewish fellowship and bond is no historical accident and that it has a purpose: elevating humanity, placing idealism above power, and bringing about a nobler and better existence for ourselves and for others. A spiritual fellowship cannot exist for nothing. It must bear fruit. . . .

3. A faith that what Jews have initiated—a fellowship built on ideals—should be followed by all other peoples. . . .

This faith in no way sets itself against either history

or science. Jewish fellowship is, without any connection to circumstances, a historical fact. That Jews were and remain bearers of lofty ideals is also a fact that only the wicked would deny. In our time Hitlerism showed that Jews are the greatest obstacle standing in the way of the wicked.

German rabbis correctly assessed Jews as a people with a mission. Without this mission the existence of the Jewish people is senseless—the Jewish bond becomes absurd. The Jewish mission does not preclude Jewish nationalism, striving for a country, a unified language, nor any other good things. This mission is merely the force that unifies Jews in times of happiness and misfortune, destruction and creation. Jews who would deny Jewish peoplehood or its mission to improve the world in reality remove themselves from Jewishness just as Americans remove themselves from Americanism when they subvert the Constitution.

Those who want to come to our acculturated young people and bring them back into the Jewish fold will never succeed if they can't point to the relation between Jewish and American ideals, to the eternal Jewish fellowship, which does not take external conditions into account, and to the inborn Jewish need to build a loftier and better life, to replace violence with freedom, vulgarity with nobility. There's a precise way to measure Jewishness. The better that Jews are in an ethical sense—the more strongly they're bonded to other Jews and the more they want to set an example for others—the more Jewish they are. The essence of the Jewish people is not only the ideal of justice but faith in spirit, in the power of the spirit over the body, in spirituality over materiality. Jews must have all of the good traits of Americans and strive even higher. We can certainly not be good Jews if we aren't good Americans in the highest sense of the word.

Relating to one of the most poignant prayers in Jewish liturgy, Singer explores divine providence and the question of whether God metes out judgment on an individual or collective basis. Setting up the problem from a theoretical perspective at first, he offers dueling ideas about the nature of God's relationship to people, then cuts through the distinction by adding a third element: the limits of our understanding about divine laws or nature. He also returns to his idea of unconscious faith as part of our everyday modern world, giving the example of paying electricity bills without knowing who or what makes our utilities work. This last detail is particularly re-markable as it relates to an item found in the Singer papers at the Harry Ransom Center in Austin, Texas: a Hebrew prayer by Singer addressed to *Ribono Shel Olam*—the Master of the Universe—handwritten on the back of an electricity bill dated March 1, 1952. The prayer was published in the original Hebrew and in English translation in *Tablet Magazine* on May 13, 2021. Singer's mention of paying an electricity bill as an act of faith in this article suggests a potential link to his personal prayer.

Philosophers and the *U'Netaneh Tokef* Prayer
(September 13, 1952)

One of the most ancient philosophical and religious questions is that of universal providence versus personal providence—that is, whether the higher powers are concerned only with the universal, the collective, or also with every single person separately.

From the Hebrew Bible, you might deduce in one direction or another. Very often the prophets speak in a tone suggesting that God rewards and punishes each person separately, as if God watched over each and every one of us. At other times the prophets use a tone suggesting that God punishes and rewards whole groups or peoples and is less concerned about whether this or that person is an innocent victim of punishment. In general the Hebrew Bible gives the impression that God keeps every single person in mind. This is why God would have refrained from destroying Sodom had ten righteous people been found. God, it seems, keeps a precise account of who has been good and who has been bad. According to the Hebrew Bible, God is all-knowing, and so there's no reason for not keeping every single person in mind.

The Talmud leans almost completely toward the idea of personal providence—a divine eye that watches over every single person. As it says, "You can't even injure your finger down below unless it's ordered from above." Forty days before people are born, orders from above decide who they will marry. With time Jews grew in their belief that everyone has an account in the heavens, that our deeds are recorded in a book, and that during the Days of Awe, between Rosh Hashanah and Yom Kippur, each person's deeds are weighed and their fate determined. It is written on Rosh Hashanah and signed on Yom Kippur. According to the Kabbalah, the entry is not finally published until Hoshana Rabbah.

A whole series of medieval Jewish philosophers, Maimonides among them, seemed unable to make peace with the idea that there was a special heavenly accounting for each person. They believed that this took the heavens for too human, too earthly. They said both openly and implicitly that it made much more sense for there to be a universal accounting in the heavens—an account that considers whole masses, just like the commander of an army determines the functions of the army and its divisions as a whole, and lets lower-ranked officers worry about each individual soldier. This writer has met deeply religious people who refused to accept any belief in such private or personal bookkeeping. It seemed too bizarre to them, too fanatical.

They had plenty of proof. There was an earthquake and an entire city crumbled unto itself. There was a war or an epidemic and millions of people died, small children among them. It's somehow hard to believe that in the heavens they would hand down a death sentence to a child. Among religious thinkers, Hitler's destruction only strengthened the conviction that God's decrees fell upon whole communities and that they had nothing to do with this or that particular person. In short, God's laws, like the laws of nature, were valid for large groups.

One thinker made the following remark: When I put money into the bank, I want it to be secure and for the bank not to go bankrupt. But I don't want the bank's director to give every one of my pennies special attention. Even if the director were a relative and started putting out reports on my few dollars, it still wouldn't bring me any more money. Another pointed to Goethe's comparison of the human soul to water. If we know the laws that govern fluids, it's easy to explain each drop of water found on the ground, in the air, in the sea, or even in a stone. If God kept a precise accounting of every single drop of water, the distribution of water could and would not be any more understandable or useful than it is already. . . .

We don't know the laws of life like we know the laws that govern fluids, which is why we can't explain the phenomena of the living world. But if people knew the laws of life, they'd be able to explain the existence of every housefly or microbe, every genius or criminal. Things would become clear and understandable, and the idea of special heavenly supervision for every moth, every worm, and even every person would appear completely redundant. If we knew the laws of life we'd understand that the words of *U'Netaneh Tokef*—about a heavenly accounting for each and every person—have a value that is not literal but poetic.

So said certain religious thinkers. How can we respond to their words?

The answer is that, as far as water is concerned, we can't make moral claims. Regardless of whether you find water in a stone, in the body of a fish, in someone's urine, or in rose petals—there can be no talk of wrongs that were done to the water, and there can be no question of justice. We presume that water does not feel, worry, or suffer, and it's all the same to the water where it's located or in what form. Water has no individuality, no personal "I." The laws of nature, nature's algebra, are completely suited to this. It would truly be redundant, from our human perspective, for there to be a separate accounting for each drop of water when these simple laws work so perfectly.

But humans suffer. Humans have a personal "I." They have will, ambition, ideals, dreams. It makes a big difference to people whether they are beggars or millionaires, sick or healthy, valued and distinguished or downtrodden. Can there be an algebra that reconciles every wrongdoing? Can there be a formula that explains the suffering of Jewish children at Majdanek, the evil of the Nazis, the anguish of innocent people who spend their lives in prison, the successes of people who do bad things for years and stay healthy and happy into old age? Can there be a law, such a universal accounting, that could respond to Job's questions and sufferings?

According to our human conception, such a law is impossible. Where there's individuality or a personal "I"—where there's suffering and joy, justice and injustice—no scientific method can be applied. . . . If water could experience happiness and unhappiness, good deeds and vile deeds, it too would compose a prayer like *U'Netaneh Tokef.* . . .

The *U'Netaneh Tokef* prayer contains the same power

and the same depth regardless of whether there's a precise account in the heavens where each person's deeds are written down, or whether life is structured such that good and evil are recorded and reconciled automatically. It doesn't matter how the accounting works. What matters is the final sum—that the numbers match up, the calculations can be backed up.

In modern times we've learned to pay bills to companies we know nothing about. We pay by check, and the people cashing it have no idea what we look like. We send the check by mail, which delivers our envelopes without knowing who or what we are. We often pay for things without knowing how they work. For example, we pay for electricity. Or else sit at home, enjoying music that a musician does not play specifically for us, which is carried to us with the help of waves about which we know nothing.

Yes, even in our little physical world, our personal "I" often comes up against powers that are greater than we are—higher and farther—powers toward which we have obligations and require precise accounting. We will perhaps never discover how the technicians of the universe do their work when it comes to such delicate things as life, justice, suffering. But we turn on the light and we have to pay our bills. This is the true reality of the *U'Netaneh Tokef*.

Singer was known for his abhorrence of all -isms—ideologies and dogmas claiming to serve human causes while limiting freedoms and individuality—yet this is one of the few articles in which he offers his alternative vision. Putting forth the idea of "cultural democracy," he makes a case for a more experiential and participatory way of engaging with creative expression, whether literature, theater, lectures, or any other artistic mode. Again comparing contemporary culture to the traditional lifestyle of the studyhouse or *shtibl*, Singer defends "simple" people from the idea that they know less than scholars or intellectuals. He says that inherited or traditional knowledge often comes together with living spaces or locations where activities take place regularly—and he foregrounds the need to cultivate close-knit, inclusive, and engaging communities in the United States.

Everyday Jews—Yesterday and Today
(October 25, 1952)

Reading the memoirs of revolutionaries, you often come across things that appear rather strange today. An important revolutionary, the leader of some great movement, gets an address for a carpenter or a shoemaker. He comes to the carpenter, who hides him, but this isn't all. The carpenter has thoughts of his own. He conducts long discussions with his guest. The memoirist often describes the differences of opinion between him and the carpenter. In those days there was not as much social distance between intellectuals and simple people. A carpenter was taken seriously. Leaders such as Leo Deutsch, Menahem Mendel Rosenbaum, Chaim Zhitlowsky, Pyotr Kropotkin, Vladimir Medem—they all found it important to convey the words of simple people in their work and to write about them as equals. In books like these you sometimes find photographs of carpenters or shoemakers wearing black shirts and high collars. There is a certain sense of pride in their faces. After all, for whom was the revolution meant but for them and their kind?

You find a similar relationship to the working class in many movements at the beginning of their development. This was the case with early Christians, the Jacobins in France, during the rise of Hasidism, the settlement of Israel, the colonization of America. When people start something, they are still idealistic, further from being snobs. Scorn for the poor comes with success. With time, everyday Jews become unnecessary. They become a source of shame—their appearance, their clothes, the way they talk. Their position increasingly falls until they become anonymous masses who have to hear out every speech, clap when leaders speak, and buy tickets to all kinds of programs. And that's where it ends. There was time and patience enough to discuss things with one carpenter, but you can't make a fuss over thousands or millions of great people.

This tragedy is even more striking when it comes to cultural movements. Our time completely lacks what I would call *cultural democracy*. The entire cultural life of our time is structured such that ordinary people are completely passive. No matter where they go, they are limited to the same activity: sitting silently in their seats. They sit quietly everywhere: at the theater, at the movies, at lectures, at all kinds of political gatherings. They are, in reality, like Y. L. Peretz's famous character Bontshe the Silent, or rather more like Bontshe the Seated. Lecturers and all kinds of performers express their thoughts—they act, sing, dance, discuss, argue. They have full, active roles. The masses always have to be in awe of them. All that's left for them to do is to smack their hands together in applause.

Were things always like this? There were times when people participated actively in such things. It's important to point out that simple Jews were quite active in religious Jewish life. They were not silent in the studyhouse—they prayed, they recited psalms, they studied. They were called up to the Torah. Different tradespeople had their own synagogues where they called the shots. Many simple Jews became Hasidim and traveled to their rebbes. They were invited to town meetings where they spoke and expressed their opinions. Simple Jews belonged to all kinds of societies: burial societies, bridal assistance, poorhouses. They cared for orphans and helped poor brides get married. Totally simple people led prayer services, if not on Rosh Hashanah and Yom Kippur then during weekdays. And when the cantor did lead services, simple Jews backed him up with song. At weddings simple Jews would tuck their kaftans up and dance until the windows rattled. It may seem strange, but in the past simple Jews were more active than Jewish scholars. Scholars sat on their behinds while simple people took action. This was completely natural and in accordance with the needs of the simple folk, who had a lot of energy, were often optimistic, had a knack for jokes, and often had physical strength. Old-time simple Jews would not have accepted being silent or keeping their opinions to themselves.

Big cities, major movements, and wide territories that separate people in a single country, along with a constant lack of time, have all stripped regular people of their active roles. Today only professional singers sing and only professional dancers dance. The privilege of performing and being funny belongs only to actors. At meetings the public is given the floor less and less. How can we have time for them? There are so many speakers! It doesn't matter whether we're celebrating a holiday, or grieving, or protesting, or demanding something—the average person remains both silent and anonymous. . . .

There were times when landsmanshaftn—societies formed by Jewish immigrants who'd come from the same shtetls or cities—gave simple Jews the opportunity to express themselves. This writer believes that landsmanshaftn still exist today thanks to the fact that everyday Jews are at least not strangers or anonymous figures there. But there's been a change in landsmanshaftn. They too are governed by increasing bureaucracy. In addition, they put on fewer shows. These societies have, to a great degree, become similar to large organizations, especially big-city societies.

This writer believes that we should build a cultural life governed less by professionals, no matter whether they are speakers, actors, singers, or dancers. Regular people know perfectly well how to speak, sing, dance, and even act and be funny. They always could in the past, and they can do it today. There was a small society that would pray in my father's little courtroom, and I remember up to this day how wonderfully they danced, sang, and discussed all kinds of issues, all without any chairperson, without any specific rules or regulations. I saw these Jews on Simhat Torah, Purim, the end of the Yom Kippur fast, and on various other occasions. On Coney Island and Miami Beach I saw simple Jews sing songs, lead interesting discussions, and enjoy themselves with a passion—with a youthful fire despite being old.

It is clear that in America the conditions for a close-knit communal life are nowhere nearly as favorable as they were in Europe. We're familiar with all of the difficulties. But if we actually want to build a cultural life here, pouring time and resources into it, it needs to be built in a way that has joy—that attracts the younger generation. . . . This grassroots Jewish cultural movement has to be planned in a way that will give regular Jewish people the chance to derive pleasure from Yiddishkayt both intellectually and emotionally. Instead of building this or that large center we have to build lots of smaller clubs. Instead of rigid programming the public should be given more initiative. Instead of talking endlessly about leadership the public should be encouraged to take part in activities that require less external guidance and use more of their own internal strengths. . . .

Jewish cultural production must take everyone into account. It cannot isolate itself in the corner. It cannot be one-sided. If we assume that our people is alive and will continue to live, we have to ensure that it isn't a dry and miserable life. . . . And why was Hasidism so successful? Because it revived Jewish vitality, because it elicited in people both ethical powers and vital forces. The two were united. In its first years Yiddishism had a lot of life. It's worth recalling *Ha'Zamir* in Warsaw, where singing, dancing, and theater went together with serious lectures. You could grab a book there or play a game of chess. You could meet new people. Every professional and Zionist organization was a place where people came together—not only leaders but the masses themselves. They set the tone. This is where the young people who built and fought for Israel grew up. The tragedy in America is that here they build movements in such a way that the office dominates. The synagogues are closed. The organizations are shuttered. People only come to meetings, and everything is already prepared. There are certainly reasons—very important ones. But at least people should know that this is a curse, not a blessing, and that resources have to be found to fight this. This office Jewishness empowers assimilation, dries up people's inner juices, and turns American Jews into an extinguished people. You see more extinguished people here than you did in Poland in the years of hunger during the German occupation of World War I or even in Hitler's ghettos.

These questions touch upon our very existence. American Jewry must be spiritually and organizationally enlivened if it doesn't want to succumb from too much silence. It will die simply because there will be no desire to live.

As in other articles in this volume, Singer here perceives a lack in the way literature is approached in the Yiddish language and highlights challenges he would soon undertake himself. He sets out the nature of the problem, which gets addressed or worked over in his literary fiction. This piece articulates another clear mission: a moral standard that would reflect on Jewish history in the modern era, at least from the Hasakalah of the early 19th century to the Holocaust of the mid-20th century—the time when he was developing his own literary path. This article is also notable because, writing under the name Yitskhok Varshavski, Singer suggests that the closest an author has come to fulfilling this kind of soul-searching is his older brother, Israel Joshua Singer, who died of a heart attack in early 1944. Singer is clearest about the need to incorporate historical consciousness into a collective moral soul-searching that reflects on Jewish life and culture over at least the last hundred years.

Yiddish Literature Does Not Portray the Great Events of Our Time

(November 2, 1952)

When I think about Yiddish literature, its strengths and faults, I always have to wonder again why it has exploited so little of the riches of Jewish life. It's strange that it hasn't portrayed a single one of the greatest political movements. The Haskalah was still blooming when Mendele Moykher Sforim started to write. Mendele was thoroughly familiar with the Haskalah. But for some reason he didn't give it the attention it deserved. Mendele found something charming in the backwardness of the shtetl, which he called *Kabtsansk* (Poorville), *Tuneyadevka* (Parasiteville), and other such names. Even in the littlest shtetls he selected those with the least spirit. He all but disregarded the Maskilim, the yeshiva boys who yearned for an education and the big city, the half-assimilated provincial doctors and pharmacists. This is also true of Sholem Aleichem, who dedicated all of his tremendous talent to the simple folk. Y. L. Peretz knew Jewish intellectuals better than any other writer, but he had no patience for large canvases. He actually wrote poetic prose, the kind in which tone and music play a central role.

It's strange, but Yiddish literature has not painted an extensive picture of immigration, the Hibbat Zion movement, Zionism, and socialism in all their varieties and variations. Tens of thousands of young Jews enrolled in universities, became doctors, lawyers, and engineers, all settling in the biggest cities of Western Europe and America. An entire country and language were resurrected before the eyes of Yiddish literature. Before its eyes Jews threw themselves into the Russian Revolution, led conspiracies, sat in all kinds of prisons, were sent to Siberia, lived through all kinds of revolutions, disappointments, protests, periods of remorse. Yiddish writers were all witnesses to the blooming of communism among our people. Yiddish writers were present as an entire people tossed off the yoke of religion and threw themselves into the secular world, with all its attractions and pitfalls. It may sound strange, but even Jewish business and industry is not sufficiently represented in our literature. Even Hasidism does not appear to the degree that it should. Where are the greatest Hasidic courts—Rizhin, Ger, Belz, Trisk, Lubavitch, and all the others? Where are our assimilationists, with all their illusions about the joys of secular life? Where is the mass immigration to America, with all its confusions and complications? We could fill an entire article with these kinds of questions.

The truth is that so much has happened in so little time that Yiddish literature hasn't had time to catch its breath. Yiddish literature, as we see it, was born in the 1870s. Like every literature, its beginnings were small and modest. It started as a spark while Jewish life was ablaze like a wildfire. In reality, all Jewish movements— the entire spiritual history of a people, with all its hopes, its ideals and deviations, its dreams and illusions—find their sharpest expression between 1870 and 1920. In these fifty years our people experienced countless dramas—both comedies and tragedies. Everything that took generations to gather went to waste in a single epoch. An entire people was ripped apart into endless factions and parties. Every combination of which the Jewish mind is capable was realized one way or another. From a people that seemed outdated and broken burst forth a powerful vitality that can be compared to no other nation. But literature was absolutely unprepared to cope with such a storm.

We know that when many contradictory stimuli befall animals—or even people—certain creatures become as if paralyzed and tend to fall into a deep sleep. Inhibition sets in, a kind of shrinking of their powers and consciousness. We suspect that this has partly happened to Yiddish literature. It has hidden in a corner mainly in order to survive. In other words, our literature has been marked by a process of contraction from the very start. Instead of opening its eyes wide to see better, it had to shade them so as not to be blinded.

The beginning of any intellectual development influences its later stages. If our first authors had to limit themselves for particular reasons, later this limitation all but became our fate. The literature attracted the kind of talent for which limits and limitations came naturally. Writers appeared who did not have to hide in a corner because they tended to be prickly people, honest but restricted in scope. What had started as a need soon became a virtue. What's more, the objective conditions began increasingly to push toward this impasse. Yiddish literature was extremely provincial, and provincials became its greatest readers and admirers. Literature neglected our intellectuals on the right and on the left—the nationalist, the assimilated, the religious scholars and secular academics—and the intellectuals consciously or unconsciously neglected our literature. This would surely not have happened to such an extent had Yiddish literature portrayed Jewish life more broadly. The literature would have then rescued the language. More than once have great authors or literary epochs put neglected languages back on their feet.

This writer does not usually deal with literary history, and he wouldn't have dealt with this topic had he not sought links between past and present.

In other literatures, writers don't feel that they have a debt to pay to this or that literary epoch. For hundreds of years, English, French, and Spanish writers portrayed the life of their people. Writers could now and then find a gap, an opportunity to write about something new. But the historical novel is far from being the essence of literature. In our case, an altogether different situation developed. Yiddish writers, especially those who write prose, have and should have guilty consciences. They've been given opportunities that no writers have been given before. Countless literary subjects have literally been sitting right in front of them. Life has been so dramatic, so loaded with material, that you'd have to be blind to overlook it. But it's a fact that Yiddish literature, on the whole, has not exploited these treasures. The exceptions can be counted on your fingers. Our guilt is even greater because our shortsightedness—and our fear of looking light and darkness in the face—has damaged the development of the Yiddish language.

Is it too late to return to what we've lost? The answer is that it isn't too late yet, but it will be soon. Yiddish writers living today have themselves experienced a great part of our lost era. They spoke its language and breathed its air. Whether the writers are young or old, they—or at least their parents—belonged to that period. They can draw directly from the source. Even if they belong to a certain camp, they have a natural understanding of the other camps. Even if they slept through that time in literary terms, they didn't sleep through it in reality. They had often themselves escaped from religious households and themselves lived through the experiences of the Haskalah. There are many of those whose parents—and who themselves—went to rebbes and who tasted the flavor of Hasidism. They have obviously immigrated, either to North America or to Israel or to South America, and they know what Jewish immigration is. The generations of writers who will come after us—whether they write in Yiddish, Hebrew, or English—will envy today's generation of writers. Even if they didn't belong to the golden age of Yiddish literature, they at least belonged to an age of Sturm und Drang—the likes of which may have never been experienced in Jewish history. The reasons that Yiddish writers have not tried, each according to their own abilities, to immortalize all of these remarkable struggles and transformations will perhaps remain a mystery for future literary historians. To a great extent, it's already a mystery now.

There is certainly no lack of diligence or readiness to work under the harshest conditions, which can be seen by the number of books that are published without the writers receiving any payment. The will is certainly there.

Is there a lack of talented writers? It's true that we don't have many. Talent is always a rare gift. But we have had and still have talented writers. I have never before written about I. J. Singer, yet he wrote a number of novels that act as partial responses to these questions. In *The Brothers Ashkenazi* he painted a portrait of Jewish business and industry. In *Yoshe Kalb* he composed a novel about Hasidism, actually about Hasidism's downfall. He portrayed Jewish immigration in *The Family Carnovsky* and Jewish communism in *East of Eden.* In his own way, he had covered a large part of modern Jewish history. Isaac Meir Weissenberg, Sholem Asch, Dovid Bergelson, Zalman Shneour, A. M. Fuchs, Y. Y. Trunk, Efraim Kaganowski, Yoshue Perle, and a whole series of other European Yiddish writers have each, in their own ways, portrayed Jewish life as they saw and witnessed it. The American Yiddish writers have surely done their part. Though it's hard to say who's American. Is Jonah Rosenfeld American? Is Lamed Shapiro American? Are David Pinski and Avrom Reyzen American? They all wrote in Europe too. One way or another you get the sense that something's been left unsaid. This era has barely been touched upon. So much has happened that has so changed the path of our history! Our literature, as a whole, has overlooked and slept through much of it. Our whole generation is like a bunch of Honi HaMe'agels— the Talmudic sage who slept for decades. We've slept for seventy years! But it's not yet too late—and that has to be mentioned at every opportunity.

The books that will be written about the last seventy or hundred years will be partly historical but partly written from personal experience. One of the most difficult obstacles for Yiddish writers in America is language. We've hardly accounted for how much Yiddish we've forgotten—and continue to forget. The words are Yiddish, but the idioms are often English. When I look at our literary journals, I'm shocked. A number of Yiddish writers think in English and translate their English-language idioms into Yiddish word for word. Very often, an English idiom pops up in a story about Jewish life in Poland or Lithuania. We have our old-world characters speak a kind of Yiddish that emerged in New York or Chicago. Nahum Stutchkoff's *Thesaurus of the Yiddish Language* can be helpful where words are concerned but not where it concerns expressions or sentence structure. Yiddish writers must, from the outset, be careful not to sin against the language. They must examine their own use of language. And they have constantly to study Yiddish. We have no Language Committee here, as they have in Israel. We still don't have a scholarly Yiddish dictionary. We have to stand up before our Yiddish philologists and file our complaint: What are they waiting for? I am thinking, first and foremost, of Dr. Max Weinreich.

But language isn't the only thing. There is in reality no comprehensive Jewish history of the last hundred years. Documents have been lost. Newspapers, books, and journals were either torn to shreds or burned. Yiddish writers often have to do the work of historians and ethnographers.

Another thing that's very important is the perspective or approach. From what viewpoint should we think about this era? Obviously, we can't dictate the perspective to anyone. But it's helpful to point out that to paint a great literary picture it's not enough to be removed in time and space. It demands an overall ideology. It demands even more of you. Writers have to be able to look truth in the eye without taking external authorities, their personal pasts, or their contemporary environments into account. Let's say things as they are: Writers must have a moral standard. They must have a personal philosophy. Without it, the facts don't stick together, and the selection of events is random.

We believe that one of the reasons that Yiddish writers have not succeeded in portraying the full scope of this great era is that they have not recognized its mistakes nor taken account of the great forces by which it has been driven. Intellectually speaking, many Yiddish writers are stuck in the Haskalah, though they don't say it openly since it's unfashionable. They forget that the same Haskalah that brought education and created Zionism and Yiddish literature had also given birth to assimilation, communism and mixed marriages, and the Jewish self-hatred that has grown to a tragic degree in our generation. Others, on the contrary, make the mistake of being unable to distinguish between actual religion and religious rhetoric, between the primeval elements of religion and its outgrowth, whose value has passed. We cannot now return to this tremendous era without undertaking some soul searching. What was good? What was bad? Where did the truth lie and where lay the mistakes? We must by now have already possessed a perspective, a moral standard. Writers have to account for their own lives, for their own obligations to God and to people, to the Jewish nation and to themselves. We believe that the lack of this kind of soul searching is largely to blame for Yiddish literature being so far behind these tremendous events. . . . We have nearly no right to come to readers with our complaints when we still owe so many debts to Yiddish literature.

Refracting his earlier theme on the unconscious faith of Jews who out-
wardly tout materialist ideologies, Singer now undertakes precisely
the kind of historical soul searching he had set out in the earlier
piece, exploring the ways that Jewish culture both distinguished
itself from its surrounding cultures and later tried to integrate into
them. He exposes what he sees as the ironic aspects of Jewish
insularism as well as the tragicomic ways that it was reversed
when Jews were emancipated and allowed to partake in mainstream European societies. The piece also stands as a warning to
Jews, especially in the United States and Israel, where everyday
secular life had the most potential of capturing both their hearts
and imaginations. He warns Jews in the postwar period against
the temptation to put all their energies into the material world and
urges them to remember that their cultural history includes spiritual
treasures too.

Jews and the World

(November 22, 1952)

For nearly two thousand years Jews have been martyrs on account of a religious truth. Jews did not want to make peace with the idea that a human being can be either God or God's son. They believed that it was worth suffering for this truth and to die in order to sanctify the name of God. Life in the material world, they argued, is short, nothing but a corridor, and the eternal palace is above, in eternity. Besides, Jews have always held the door wide open for those who didn't agree with them. Jews never sought converts. Anyone who wanted to convert to Christianity was free to do so. Jews asked just one thing of apostates: not to denounce their people or to provoke others against them.

These Jews did not get involved in worldly matters. Jews needed to earn a living, but they were neutral in every war, uprising, and various conflicts between all the different princes, dukes, and whatever else they liked to be called. Old-time Jews had no relation to the rewards or happiness of this world. This was true partly until my time. My own father had no relation to political events. It made no difference to him whether World War I would be won by the Russians or the Germans. He had no interest in the constitution, the parliament, the Polish-Soviet war, or any other worldly developments. He would say, "What does it matter to me whether this goy is in power or another?" For him, "goys" included secular Jews. He wouldn't even become a member of Agudat Yisrael, which started out as a political party representing Orthodox Jews in Poland. For him, something about it was unjewish.

I mention my father because he represented Jews of the past in my own time.

Emancipation gave Jews civil rights, and Western European Jews changed their relation to the material world as early as the first years of the 19th century. This world was no longer a corridor for them, and they began considering this earth and the world around them as the real palace. All of the good things that can happen to people can happen here and nowhere else. If there's no happiness in *this* world, there will certainly be no happiness deep in the earth or up in the heavens. The Haskalah relayed this message to Eastern Europe in a thousand different ways.

When Jews took on this worldview, they suddenly felt extremely helpless and desperate. First, it meant that we'd suffered senselessly for generations. But this wasn't the main thing, since we're not usually too worried about the past. The bigger trouble was that Jews were inadequately armed for the future. They were physically weak, spoke a language unrecognized by others, had no right to live where they wanted or to educate their children. They had no land. In their minds they became worldly, but their bodies and their circumstances were somehow not of this world.

The solution was then to catch up with everything they had neglected and missed over so many generations.

And Jews started catching up.

They spoke Yiddish, but they quickly learned to speak other languages. They took off their long garments. They began studying at all the universities. They straightened out their postures and started enjoying nature, love, art, and all the other good things. They quickly realized that they had to have political influence, to take part in international struggles and battles, since now, as worldly people, all of these questions pertained to them too. They had to take sides and let people hear what they had to say.

The speed with which Jews caught up with the world they had missed was truly astonishing. A yeshiva student who had barely left the study house cut off his sidelocks and could soon speak the local language, and his grammar was better than the average local's. He studied quickly, read a lot, and learned thousands of detailed facts. He was soon as much a specialist of the material world as he had been of the world to come. He discovered that his neighbors were backward. He began to put pressure not only on himself but also on his neighbors. Here was the world—so why were they sleeping? Let's build this world together for us, for you, for the future, for every class and social position. Jews began to join parliaments and political parties. Some of them wanted a country, some sort of territory. All of today's movements, with all of their variations and particularities, came into being.

The non-Jewish world was stunned. It was difficult to grasp how yesterday's slackers, who had completely ignored the material world, suddenly became so passionate, so infatuated with the earth, with all its fortunes and misfortunes. Jewish participation in the press, in the theater, in literature, in every other aspect of civilization and literature was tremendous. This momentum incited considerable envy, fear, hate, and very often also astonishment.

A very small number of Jewish thinkers, who can literally be counted on the fingers of one hand, saw that everything was not as it should be. People who study too quickly can often make major mistakes and often can't penetrate the essence of what they've studied. Something wasn't right about the young Jewish prodigy who had learned everything about the non-Jewish world in one fell swoop.

What wasn't right? A few things.

First, it is generally not healthy to hurry and push this way. Students can skip one class, maybe two, but when they skip *all* their classes, hopping from one university to another, it raises suspicion. We worry about their minds. We suspect that they aren't studying as well as they should. We worry about their health. Everyone knows that wonder kids often slip up and lead to considerable disappointment.

Second, people noticed that Jews dedicated too much religious devotion to the material world. The same piety that they showed at the studyhouse, reciting psalms or getting up in the middle of the night to lament the destruction of Jerusalem, was now applied to worldly matters. They surrounded everyday things with holiness. They brought their religious ecstasy to subjects that demanded composure, cold reason, skepticism. And here the mistake was only on the surface. It was not just a matter of making a mistake. Jews had also made themselves laughable. They had shown that they had not properly digested their new scripture.

Third, Jews underestimated the realities of earthly powers. When it comes to heavenly matters, you can go forth with all your might. But the earth is full of circumstances, oppositions, interests, and simple indolence and indifference, which aren't so easily moved aside. With their momentum, modern Jews often knocked their heads right up against stone walls. This way, Jews revealed a remarkable lack of national egoism. Every time they hit someone else once, they hit themselves ten times. They made countless enemies. They transferred their religious martyrdom to a realm where martyrdom isn't justified. Jews had, in their typically Jewish way, started transforming this world into the world to come. They had mixed everything up.

Fourth, in their race to transform the hallway into a palace, Jews began ridding themselves of their distinctive traits, wiping away their appearance and whatever made them unique. They began increasingly to imitate others, to assimilate, and there arose a danger that they would end up standing naked at the marketplace of the nations, with neither faith in the world to come nor clothes for this world. Friendly warnings were voiced that Jews had, unfortunately, very often bitterly and unjustly denounced things without fully understanding or appreciating them.

The essence of every warning was: Don't rush, Mr. Israel! Don't get so excited! It's not good for Grandpa Israel, the old Israel, to be so wildly infatuated with the material world! He doesn't have the strength to change things all at once! It's ridiculous to be so religious about things that are so mundane. Think things through, act slowly, don't start wars you can't win, and don't sacrifice yourself for other people's idols. The material world demands composure, not hysteria. And, the main thing, don't throw away the old and the time-proven for the sake of something that's still unfamiliar and unknown to you. Don't throw away the fortune you've collected over four thousand years for projects that amount to nothing. It's not enough, Mr. Israel, to have a mind on fire and a burning desire. You also have to control yourself.

Modern Jews rejected these warnings and still reject them to this day because they don't agree with their temperament. Jews are believers by nature. They need to believe, and when they do, a fire is ignited inside them. But some fires have to be tamed. Some fevers have to be treated with ice. Our souls can bear astronomical temperatures, but our bodies, our worldly selves, cannot be either too hot or too cold. As soon as Jews plunge into matters of the body, corporeal pleasures and hopes, they have to learn to keep their balance. They have to be able to think—not just for a minute but for long periods in advance, and not just about ourselves and our own moods but about the general public. Because in the world of souls, we really are separate beings—Moses is Moses and Korah is Korah. But in the corporeal world, Moses suffers for Korah's sins.

So how can a fire turn lukewarm?

The answer is that if Jews are by nature angels or seraphs, if they have to be like fire and flame, they should burn their fire out in the spiritual world. They have to do what their forebears did: be angels at synagogue and merchants at the marketplace rather than be merchants at synagogue and angels at the marketplace.

If Y. L. Peretz, Hayim Nahman Bialik, Aaron Zeitlin, and Nathan Birnbaum called to return to the studyhouse, it was because they realized that Jews had an internal fire that's of no use out on the street. Not every one of these thinkers came up with a way to account for this situation. But at certain moments they each sense that the Talmudists, the Kabbalists, the tsaddikim, and all of the saintly self-sacrificers—that they would never fit in a system where people lived by the minute and sought short-lived success. It is a question of uncontrollable forces. The marketplace is ruled by dialectics. What's good today is bad tomorrow, what's strong today is weak tomorrow. There, might literally makes right. There, people dance on graves—one person's pleasure is another's pain. And you certainly have to be both honest and careful there. In the marketplace, the righteous and the wicked each behave according to their own principles. But placing all your hopes in the stock market, pouring your whole soul into it, dying for it—this is foolish, crazy, perverse.

Jews were not created to place all their hopes on human beings, on political flip-flopping, on this dubious world, on temporary victories. Jews have an internal fire that strives for eternity, for the lofty and the good, for the spheres that are not ruled by competition, lies, greed, contradictions, or falsities. If Jews had a corner where they could live spiritually, they wouldn't be so hot on the marketplace. They would be neither too hot nor too cold. They wouldn't want to outdo other nations in their worldliness or kill for this or that project. They would see things clearly and act correctly. If Jews were spiritually able to live their lives the right way, it would help them in this world too.

Jews have been left with a great spiritual legacy. They can't use the legacy in its entirety, but there's plenty to choose from. The modern Jews' biggest problem is spiritual in nature. If they find a spiritual home, faith in higher matters, moral principles, Jewish warmth—then they'll be calmer when it comes to human matters. If not they'll stay overexcited and make greater and greater mistakes by the day. Many Jewish catastrophes in modern history are rooted in this very state of overexcitement. You can pray with passion, with a loud voice, with your hands raised up to the skies, but you can't make such gestures when you play chess or politics.

The Jewish thorn bush, its burning bush, can only stay ablaze without burning out when it burns with a sacred fire. When this Jewish fire turns into an everyday furnace, Jews get burned, their values burn out, and the people are transformed into one big misunderstanding among the nations.

Unlike all of the other articles in this and the previous volume, which appeared under the name Yitskhok Varshavski, this article was published under the name D. Segal, a pseudonym Singer used mostly for his more sensational or uncouth pieces—though one that he also used for literary experiments and personal writings that had a more ironic tone than his other work. This appears to be one of the earliest autobiographical pieces he had written about his life as a young man, referring, in this case, to the winter of 1922-1923, which he spent in the small Galician shtetl of Stary Dzików—then in the Lwow region of Poland and today on the border of Ukraine—where his father had been rabbi since the middle of World War I. This was the place where Singer spent his last months living a traditional lifestyle, having left the Tachkemoni Religious Seminary in Warsaw in the middle of the school year to live with his parents and youngest brother Moyshe. From there he left religion behind and embarked on his career as a young writer and intellectual.

Small Shtetl, Big Swamp

(January 29, 1953)

There's a Yiddish saying: *We should be spared what we can learn to endure.*

People living in big cities, surrounded by movies, theaters, concerts, and every other form of entertainment, sometimes feel that if they were forced to sit in some far-off farm, they'd die of boredom. But the people who sit on that farm have gotten used to the monotony of their lives. When they come to the big city, the hustle and bustle makes them so tired they just can't understand how people live with so much commotion in their lives.

When I think of the monotony of the Jewish shtetl in Poland or Lithuania just a few decades ago I start to shudder. In my personal opinion it was worse than a prison.

Theaters and movies were out of the question. But they didn't even have books. No newspapers made it there. You saw the same people every day and said the same things to them. They made a big fuss over the smallest things. A cow gave birth to a calf. A hen started crowing and they slaughtered it. The bath attendant got drunk. You often had to listen to the same silly story from a number of different people. You listened out of politeness and because you did need something to talk about.

I once spent a winter in a tiny shtetl in eastern Galicia, the kind where, when a carriage comes into town, the horse's head is at one end of the town and the back wheels at the other end. This shtetl was not only small but unusually backward, and it also had muddy swamps that were rare even for Eastern Galicia. It lay in a valley, and all of the water from the whole region collected there. It was the first time in my life that I saw old women and even young girls walking around in men's boots. Between the end of Sukkot and around the time of Shavuot, no one there wore shoes.

The only place in the shtetl people could get together was the studyhouse. But it was a tiny little place, and there was not a living soul there all day. It didn't even have enough religious books to study. There were a few copies of the Gemara, the Mishnah, a couple Hebrew Bibles, plus a single Midrash—that's all. The Jews in this shtetl owned land and were in reality half-peasants. The little houses were old, falling over, nearly in ruins.

I was then already a budding writer, though I hadn't yet seen my name in print. I had already read a lot of good and interesting books, I had spent much of my life in Warsaw, and here I was thrown into a wasteland—a godforsaken place.

I started looking for some other young person with whom I could talk or play chess, but I soon realized that this place had no such thing. The young men all walked around in muddy broad-brimmed hats and peasant boots, their sidelocks tied up together. They were uneducated and strictly religious. The girls all busied themselves with housework. It may seem like an exaggeration, but this shtetl had no connection to modern times. It seemed generally not to belong to any era. It was cut off from any culture.

About ten miles away there was a slightly bigger shtetl, just as godforsaken, which, for those of my shtetl, was like Paris. Getting there was a bitter journey. You sank in mud the entire way. And when you finally got there, there was nowhere to go and nothing to do—I mean for me, not for them. The Jews in my shtetl had only one form of entertainment, "legal action," which is how they referred to filing an official complaint against someone.

People would have an argument and then bring their dispute to court. The shtetl had a "Kultus President," who was actually just the synagogue's caretaker, and this Kultus President instigated all kinds of disputes and trials. Every Monday and Thursday he was served a "*termin*," a summons to appear at court. The judge knew both the Kultus President and his enemies well. He also knew Yiddish. He had to determine whether the word *sheygets* was an insult or not or whether it was an insult to call someone up to read *toykheykhe*, the Torah portion that lists the punishments Jews incur for abandoning God's path. Usually the judge would suggest some sort of compromise. This constant legal action cost both money and trouble. But people did need something to do.

When two Jews had to go to court, they hired a carriage together. Why hire two carriages and pay twice the amount? Because the carriage had to leave at daybreak, one of the men would go and wake the other. The same Kultus President who called someone a *sheygets* or low-life had to go and bang on the window of the man who brought legal action against him.

"Hey, Moyshe-Mendl, the carriage is waiting!"

And Moyshe-Mendl crawled out from under his featherbed and went with the Kultus President to bring legal action.

On the way, they were quiet for a bit, but how long can two Jews stay quiet?

"You know, Yakosh, I heard that the price of onions is rising," said the Kultus President, trying to start up a conversation.

And this way they talked about onions until they reached the courthouse.

This is the kind of shtetl in which I wound up. I don't know why, but it never stopped raining or snowing there. The days were as gray as lead and stretched on like long fasts. I yearned for a book like a hungry person yearning for bread. I knew that the world had writers like Heinrich Heine, Guy de Maupassant, and Leo Tolstoy, but in this shtetl all human culture seemed like a bad dream.

Not far from the little house where I lived was a shoemaker whose daughter was as beautiful as a painting. I had my eye on her, but in that shtetl they had literally never heard of love. Everyone got married through the matchmaker. This beauty walked around in a pair of men's boots with a shawl over her head, and as far as I could see she couldn't care less about love. Her mind was asleep and her senses were paralyzed. Even Rudolph Valentino would have made no impression on her.

Suddenly there was a commotion in town. A beggar had appeared from Tarnów with fiery black eyes, a pitch-black beard, and a big stick in his hands. The beggar went around town asking for money, smelling and sniffing around everywhere, and even started a love affair with a widow. He brought life into the shtetl—lust, love, greed. He told endless lies. He made himself into a hero. He awakened the sleepy shtetl.

The widow was captivated by this worldly man and stood with him under the huppah. They had only known each other a week. After the wedding he went over to the widow's to sleep. But he hadn't taken the boss into account. The widow had a ten-year-old son, a lowlife bastard, a real bad seed. He didn't like his mother's new husband. When the woman lay with her husband in the dark making fiery love, he poured the slop pail onto them. He told his mother he'd set the house on fire and stab her and the man with a knife if she didn't send him packing. He caused so much trouble that his mother and her beggar started making love in the bathhouse.

The bath attendant caught on and made a stink. A war of words erupted throughout the shtetl. When the beggar saw that things weren't going well, he put his bag on his shoulder, took his big stick in his hand, and left, turning the widow into an *aguna*. In the meantime the Jews in the shtetl were all fighting and bringing legal action. The judge was assured of plenty of work for months.

In the middle of all this I had a good stroke of luck. I got a letter from Perets Markish and Melech Ravitch asking me to come to Warsaw and be a proofreader for the *Literarishe bleter*, the literary journal they co-edited. Today, this doesn't seem like a big event. But the move from this shtetl to the *Literarishe bleter* was enormous. I got a few issues of the journal with the letter. There was an article in there by Aaron Zeitlin. He had, as far as I remember, many grievances about European culture. He tore rationalism, realism, and naturalism completely apart. This kind of talk looked very bizarre to my eyes—as if it had come from another planet. It was like someone who spent the winter sleeping in a park reading a critique of the Waldorf Astoria not being comfortable enough or sufficiently equipped with modern conveniences.

I was overjoyed and wanted to leave the shtetl as quickly as possible. I was afraid that the folks in Warsaw might regret their offer or that there would suddenly be a train strike—or that the earth would split and there could grow, between the shtetl and Warsaw, a fiery mountain that couldn't be climbed or an abyss that couldn't be crossed. Who knew? The earth could be torn apart and my shtetl could be turned into a little planet all its own. Everything is possible.

Yes, I was in a hurry, but I'd given my clothes to a washerwoman who had hung my clothes to dry in the attic, and the roof had been cracked and the clothes were still wet. I had holes in my shoes, but it took forever for them to make shoes around there. They dragged things on while my letter from Warsaw grew tattered and lost its reality.

I went to my neighbor, the shoemaker, and asked, "What's with my shoes?"

He looked at me and said, "Today's a happy day for me. I don't have any time for your shoes."

"Why so happy?"

"I'm drawing up a marriage contract for my daughter."

I looked inside: his beautiful daughter was busy with

a shovel around the stove.

"Who's the groom?"

"Who else should he be? Also a shoemaker."

"Where are they going to live?"

"What do you mean, where? Here in the alcove."

I looked at the young woman. Her face beamed. I thought, *Is this possible? Can anyone be happy in this wasteland? Can a young woman find any joy living with a shoemaker in this little corner? What could she expect here? Mud, a shoemaker's last, peasant boots—and then being pregnant, giving birth, breastfeeding, dragging herself around with her whining brood.* In my opinion, this young woman should have taken a knife and slit her wrists. But she was full of joy.

We spoke for the first time.

"So you're *really* going to Warsaw?"

"Yup. Going to Warsaw."

"So you're *actually* going to Warsaw?"

A few days later I got into a carriage. The Kultus President was sitting in there with some of his enemies. They were going to deal with legal action. The former widow was also there. She was going to look for the beggar who had left her an *aguna.*

A few months later I was bored of the *Literarishe bleter.* I myself started delivering a few harsh words about naturalism and rationalism. I discovered that the boy who had thrown the beggar out of his mother's bed had acted according to Freud's theories. He was, in his own way, a real Freudian.

For a while I believed that no place could be as god-forsaken as the shtetl I've described. But soon thereafter Perets Markish left for an even worse wasteland—one from which there was no return. When that place's Kultus President gets into an argument with someone, he simply cuts off his head. The judges in this wasteland know no compromise. It always makes me sad to think that the man who saved me from the swamp crawled straight into a mire. No matter how deep a swamp may be, there always seems to be one that's deeper, bigger, and thicker.

And no matter how thick a swamp may be, there's always a shoemaker's daughter who's happy. If there weren't, the human race would have died out long ago.

Continuing his theme of starting from the beginning, thirty years after leaving his religious lifestyle behind in Stary Dzików—having covered the concepts of wicked and righteous as well as rule of law—Singer now tackles the concept of beauty in Jewish tradition. He focuses on the element of action in Jewish ritual and the custom of incorporating beauty into the objects used for religious practice, known in Hebrew as *tashmishei kedusha*—emphasizing their purpose rather than the objects themselves. In this sense he draws a distinction between a Jewish viewpoint that sees beauty in the way that something is done—whether the thing in question is a physical object or a thought process—and the beauty of the result or conclusion of that action. This puts emphasis on the intention involved in any given action, another core Jewish concept on which he expounds in a separate article.

The Concept of Beauty among Olden Jews

(September 5, 1953)

It's a presumed fact that art and Judaism make strange bedfellows. Noah's son Shem, the Jew, preached morality, while Japheth, the Greek, created beautiful objects. This opinion is particularly supported by the fact that no sculptures have been found in the Land of Israel. Ancient Jewish history features no great painters or sculptors. We had no theater. The Torah prohibits painting people or any other images, whether they represent humans, animals, or even fish. The Talmud includes harsh words against those who build or attend theaters. It is therefore all but confirmed that ancient Jews forbade art and considered it to be like a sin.

Some people go even further and assert that Jews are not artistic by nature. They admit that Jews have great philosophers and scientists. Figures like Baruch Spinoza, Karl Marx, Sigmund Freud, Henri Bergson, or Albert Einstein can't be waved away. But who are the Jewish artists? The greatest of them is Heinrich Heine, and people have different opinions about him. As Heine is to poetry so Felix Mendelssohn is to music. He's not one of the greatest. He doesn't compare to Bach or Beethoven. So it's not hard to dismiss Jewish artistic skill. This has been done by both antisemites and those who don't approach the issue with any sense of hate but rather seemingly conduct their research objectively.

You could write a whole book on this topic. But the mistakes and misunderstandings can also be pointed out in shorter form.

First, there is no prohibition on Jews creating beautiful things. The fact that Jews built a Mishkan—a holy tabernacle—as well as a First and Second Temple in Jerusalem shows that beauty was an important part of the Jewish religion. Even in exile, Jews tried with all their might to make their mitzvahs beautiful and to lead beautiful lives. Jews were constantly being reproached for dressing too well and for their wives wearing too much jewelry and arousing envy among their neighbors. According to the Kabbalah, beauty, or *tiferet*, is one of God's most important attributes, one of the ten *sefirot*. Museums are full of magnificent Hanukkah candelabras, Torah crowns, pointers, and breastplates, havdalah spice boxes, kiddush cups, silver trays used for *pidyon ha-ben*, the ritual of redeeming the firstborn son, all kinds of candlesticks and menorahs, and countless other beautiful things like seder plates, etrog boxes, matzah bags, megilah cases, intricately carved holy arks, Torah scroll handles, beautiful hallah knives and covers, tefillin cases, and other religious objects. If you take into account that Jews were hounded and harassed and that they were robbed and raided every other day, you have to wonder about how powerfully Jews were inclined toward beauty. The Gemara even obligated Jews to make their mitzvahs beautiful. This is based on the words, *ze Eli v'anvehu*, "this is my God, Whom I will adorn." It's interesting that very ugly things were not allowed to be touched on Shabbat or holidays because they were *muktzeh*, off limits, due to their ugliness—they were so ugly that people were not prepared to use them on such festive days.

Second, it's important to point out that for non-Jews, and especially for Europeans, the concept of art is relatively standardized, defined once and for all, and mainly taken from Greek culture. The assumption is that artists have either to compose poetry, or paint, or carve, or act, or sing. There are nine muses, and they themselves are supposed to comprise all artistic possibilities. In reality, these are rather limited concepts. In Hasidic religious books, for example, you find oceans full of poetry, though according to Greek and Latin concepts of style it isn't poetic at all. The "defects" of this poetry actually consist in their being highly original, deeply individual, and not based on any existing stylistic model. Jewish songs have the same "defects." They can't quite fit the conventional models. They have a style of their own. The genius and the beauty in our vast literature of Talmudic hair-splitting is completely unsuited to the European spirit. There's no educator who can get across to modern people the depth and beauty of a single page from Rabbi Aryeh Gintsburg's *Sha'agat Aryeh*, *The Roar of the Lion*, or the responsa of Rabbi Akiva Eiger. We should point out here that though all European critics and cultural thinkers praise originality to the skies, this same originality has to fit into the prefabricated forms and shapes of Greek and Roman culture. When people are truly original—that is, in reality completely distinct and thoroughly different—they are either neglected or avoided. This happens, moreover, not only with works by Jewish artists but also by Hindu, Arab, and many other

Middle Eastern, Asian, and African artists who do not produce according to the European model.

We can say that Europe does demand originality, but it has to be the kind of "originality" that fits a mold. Or, as the French say, the more things change, the more they stay the same. The so-called Aryan nations never really had patience for true originality. This is why poetry has gotten stuck and why modern drama and comedy is not very different from Aristophanes, and it's also why modern sculpture is little more than a repetition of the sculptors who worked more than two thousand years ago in Athens and Rome.

The main difference between the concept of beauty for Europeans and for ancient Jews is that Greeks and Romans created beautiful things that were not closely related either to the artist or to the audience. People who sculpted beautiful statues did not have to lead beautiful lives. The people who admired these statues also thought of them as a thing apart. Someone made it and now it's here. You take a look and move on. Jews put beauty into life itself. They created the highest art of all the arts: the art of living life beautifully. It was a kind of art that leaves no trace, neither bronze nor stone nor canvas. It was an art that could not stand inanimately in a museum to be viewed by tourists and schoolchildren. . . .

The beauty of the ancient Jews and the beauty of modern people are completely different. For us, beauty was deeply tied to leading a beautiful life. A curtain is only beautiful when it's a parochet that hangs on the holy ark, which brings people together to pray and kiss the Torah. The same parochet hanging in a museum and labeled with a number is no longer beautiful to Jews. A piece of velvet with golden thread is not beautiful for them, just like a bronze figure, a ceramic nude, songs sung by a scoundrel to another man's wife, or two other scoundrels who duel over some undeserving woman are not beautiful. A book stops being beautiful when it fails to teach us something. Studying loses its value when we don't pay attention to what we've learned. The most beautiful words are ugly when they aren't spoken with a whole heart and good intentions. For olden Jews, the concepts of beauty and ugliness were so different from those of non-Jews that they could hardly understand each other.

When the Haskalah arrived, enlightened Jews started looking within their own culture for the kind of beauty that Europe had created—and they were very disappointed. There was little with which to show up! Some criticized their own people bitterly. Others took to collecting remnants. Every synagogue established some kind of museum. They jumped at the medieval Jewish poets. They discovered Rabbi Yehuda Halevi, Rabbi Abraham ibn Ezra, and every other Jewish artist who was like the Europeans. Later they started photographing synagogues and gravestones. They also started looking at the ancestry of world-renowned artists. And they were proud if some Christian artist had a Jewish grandfather or grandmother. In short, they started looking for all of those points that connected us with European culture. At the same time, they presumed that whatever made us different *in reality* was wild and uncultured. In other words, we ignored and set aside our own originality. We were only good when we imitated our neighbors.

A truly Jewish aesthetic has not yet been discovered. Even if it were discovered, it would be so immensely difficult to portray. We all know that "beautiful Jews" never had to be beautiful. They could have humps in front and behind and still be beautiful. As it says in *Eshet Hayil*, a poem about female valor, "Charm is a lie, and beauty is vanity." A woman from a "beautiful home" could have lived in a half-broken hut. A beautiful house depended only on the family's ancestry. A beautiful explanation, a beautiful insight, a beautiful speech, a beautiful community, a beautiful deed—none of them had any connection with what Europeans call beautiful.

For olden Jews, it was the *kavanah*—the living person's intention—that determined whether an action was good or bad, beautiful or ugly. There is no good without a good intention, and there can exist no beauty without a beautiful intention. It's all a question of one's attitude. The gold that was used to build the Mishkan was beautiful. The gold that was used to forge the Golden Calf was revoltingly ugly. The knife with which you cut the hallah on Shabbat can be beautiful, but a dagger with which you stab someone is ugly even if it has a gold diamond-studded handle.

It will take a long time to make people understand that what counts is the *intention* behind each action, undertaking, or creative effort. Who knows how long it will take before it becomes clear to people today that the very same reforms, laws, or institutions can be good when they're undertaken with good intentions by good people and bad when they're undertaken by the wicked with bad intentions. The tragedy of all revolutions consists in their having been quickly overtaken by bad intentions—pursued out of envy and hate rather than love and justice. The ineffectiveness of European art actually lies in its being made for money and fame, not with higher intentions. There's a natural law that olden Jews discovered and that the world neither knows nor wants to know: intention is the soul, the essence, the life of every single thing.

This piece, similarly appearing under the name D. Segal like the one about the shtetl where he lived for a winter with his parents, can be seen as a pilot of sorts for the memoir series that came to be known in English as *In My Father's Court* (1966)—which first appeared under the name Yitskhok Varshavski on February 18, 1955, just three months later. Interestingly, the original Yiddish title of this piece, "Bay mayn tatn in bezdn shtub," differs slightly from the title of the series, "In mayn foters bezdn shtub"—using different prepositions as well as two different words for father. The original Yiddish title of the collected memoir that appeared in Yiddish in 1956, *Mayn tatns bezdn shtub*, was closer to the D. Segal piece than the Varshavski series and also included pieces from the continuation of the series, which appeared under the title "In mayn zeydens bezdn shtub," or "In My Grandfather's Court," starting on October 1, 1955. This piece differs from an earlier one, "Religious Questions, Rulings, Divorces, and Weddings from a Rabbinical Court in Poland" (August 13, 1944), which also described his father's courtroom, in that the earlier piece did not identify the writer as the rabbi's son. Another interesting detail consists in the earlier piece being published just months after Singer's older brother Israel Joshua Singer passed away in New York and this later piece appearing just months after his older sister Esther Singer Kreitman—the only member of his nuclear family to have lived beyond the years of World War II—passed away in London. Like the piece on Stary Dzików, also published under the name D. Segal, we see the beginnings of Singer's literary technique of blending fiction and memoir—using his personal life experience to create literary works with an artistic vision informed by all of the themes and challenges he was simultaneously working out in his nonfiction writings.

In My Father's Courtroom
(November 25, 1954)

It seems that the rabbis of America's movement of Conservative Judaism have decided that they've been conservative long enough. The time has come to be a little more reformist, and they've come up with a new idea: to reform our ancient ketubah, or marriage contract. Namely, to add a clause saying that every couple commits to going to a beit din, or rabbinical court, before they decide to get officially divorced, and to follow the judgment of the beit din.

The Orthodox rabbis were right to cry out. According to religious law, nothing should be added to the Torah, just as nothing should be removed. That's one thing. The other thing—and this is something I'm saying myself—is that American men are far from being inclined to take on new burdens. It's enough that they have to go to Reno or to another state to get divorced. It's enough that they have to pay alimony. Who would want, after all this, to commit to going to a beit din full of rabbis? The Conservative and Reform rabbis will only lead young American Jews, one and all, to turn Orthodox ahead of their wedding. From a business standpoint, this is only good for the Orthodox rabbis.

This debate about the beit din reminded me of another beit din, my father's rabbinical courtroom in Warsaw. The Jews of Krochmalna Street came to our beit din without ever committing to it in their ketubah. They came to get married, divorced, released from an engagement contract, and simply to complain about their life at home or work, their inheritance, and who knows what else. The main room of our apartment at Krochmalna 10 and later at Krochmalna 12 functioned as a court, and, believe me, it was better and quicker than the official courts. I often marveled how my father, who didn't do much otherwise, could deal with these kinds of issues.

Coming to this court didn't involve any official petitions or revenue stamps. There was no need for lawyers. Neither did you need to wait weeks or months to get a summons to appear. When two people had a conflict, they went straight to my father at that very minute— speaking their hearts and venting their anger. If our neighbors had courtrooms like these they would be unable to keep so many wrongs silent.

My father had no power. He didn't even belong to the class of rabbis known as *morei hora'a*, who got a salary from the Jewish community paid out of its own dues. His only weapon was a red handkerchief that stank of tobacco. When both litigants had finished, my father would hold out his handkerchief for them to each grab an end and he'd say, "Confirm the contract." It was a kind of guarantee that they would stand by his judgment.

And I know they stood by it. I once saw someone gnashing their teeth while hitting the table and yelling that my father had given the wrong ruling. But there was never any talk of not standing by the judgment.

People often stormed into the courtroom. We could often hear them while they were still coming up the stairs.

Our kitchen door would slam open and two men would ask in one voice, "Is the rabbi here?"

"Sorry, in the other room," my mother would answer, herself the daughter of a rabbi.

In the other room, my father sat with his religious books, studying and noting his new insights. The first thing he'd do was say, "Welcome." Then he'd ask them to sit down. Then he always asked the same question: "Who's lodging the complaint? Who's suing whom?"

The ones lodging the complaint spoke first. Often they didn't speak but yell, yet father never let the other person cut them off. He'd say, "You'll speak later. Don't worry. I'll hear both sides out. You'll speak as long as you want." And some of the time my father would say, "There are no Cossacks in my home," which meant that the person had nothing to fear. Everything was based on goodwill. These words, uttered by this man with his red beard and his long sidelocks, would calm their stormy spirits. Because religious Jews despised Cossacks and every other symbol of power.

My mother was always afraid that my father wouldn't know how to rule. How can he understand anything about business when he sits night and day studying the Gemara? I had grown up a little by then and didn't have a lot of trust in my father's practical understanding either. The street and the marketplace were completely foreign to him. He sometimes questioned people at length about things that six-year-old children already knew. He constantly told the person speaking, "Slowly!"

And so slowly he listened to both sides. When the first side wanted to speak again, the person spoke, and again the second side answered. My father's rule was not to stop anyone from speaking. He let people speak and yell and rage for so long that they both got tired. Then there came a moment when both were quiet.

This was when my father would take out his handkerchief and say, "Confirm the contract." Both people would then touch the handkerchief, and this meant they both agreed to follow my father's judgment.

Sometimes my father would ask, "How would you like me to make my judgment? Purely on the basis of the law? Or with a compromise in mind?" Jews were afraid of a "pure" judgment since it often involved some oath or written settlement. Most of them wanted a compromise.

My father's compromises were so simple that I was often ashamed of them. Most of the time he passed a judgment of fifty-fifty. This was a template, an accepted model. The person suing demanded twenty rubles. The other person said he owed him nothing. My father said he should give him ten.

I often thought that my father could have offered a more incisive judgment had he understood the situation better. But the litigants were almost always happy. It's amazing how this one outcome could calm the stormiest spirits in so many different cases. It wasn't the ruling itself that was so appropriate but rather giving both sides an equal chance. It was as if this ruling had said, "I trust you both equally, I value you both equally, and since you two have a disagreement, you have to divide it up equally."

At first the two men would grumble and look at my father a little angrily, as if silently asking him, "What did you pull off here?" But they soon calmed down and their moods improved. First of all, both sides preserved something. Second, the dispute was over. Peaceable people don't like to draw out conflicts. They don't want to keep their anger in their hearts. It's not good for their health, it doesn't help business, and it's bad for the Jews.

"Well, that's that!" one of the men would say. "If this is what the rabbi says, then that's how it'll be. Though I've lost ten rubles."

"I lost ten rubles too," the other man would say.

"You'll make ends meet with help from above," my father would say. "*He* can surely help you make up for your loss." I don't need to say that he was referring to God.

And the men would leave, wishing my father the best of health.

How complicated the whole thing would have been had they gone to court! Their few rubles would have been eaten up by lawyers and revenue stamps. The person who lost the case would have had to pay both their expenses. They would have wasted a day or two on this heartache. And on top of all this, they would have had to speak Russian, which they barely spoke. They would have also had to swear on a Christian Bible. The very thought of going to court made such people shudder. The official court was literally unkosher, cruel, deaf to real justice, slow, and full of contempt toward the litigants. It was an unjewish court. It was ruled by lies, power, and the sword. In my father's courtroom, the Jewish spirit was calmed, restored. There was a holy ark there and shelves full of religious books. It was ruled not by a gun but by a handkerchief.

The wealthy official rabbis all had assistants. But how could an unofficial rabbi afford to hire an assistant? So as the rabbi's son, I was his assistant. Hundreds of times I had to open the door to someone's house and say, "You've been called to court!" And though I was a little boy, still in heder, and usually people barely paid attention to me, these words would always arouse a kind of silence and respect. At that moment I was no longer a little brat with disheveled sidelocks in an unbuttoned coat but a court messenger. I came with a summons from the highest authority: the Torah.

All kinds of Jews—big, heavy, with angry eyes and with dark beards—set aside their business, housework, even their meals to follow me, quietly grumbling. Did they have a choice? Even the street kids, who usually threw stones at me, pulled one of my sidelocks, or called me all kinds of names, this time looked at me with respect.

Very often I would have to call a bride whose groom called her to court or a woman whose husband wanted a divorce. Walking with a young bride through the street was somewhat of a sensation for others, and for me too. Sometimes the young woman would spill her guts to me. "What does he want from me? I don't love him. Can someone *make* me love him? I don't like him anymore." This is how the bride spoke to me, a young woman with a coat, high-heeled shoes, and her hair up in a bun. There was no question of my answering her. My face was all red. I got a taste of real life, the secret of adulthood. Yes, I understood. How can you summon someone who no longer loves you to court? Can the Torah make them love you?

But why didn't she love him? I had already seen the young groom. He had such a nice little mustache. He wore a stiff hat and a paper collar. He spoke to my father in such a heartfelt way. Now I was walking too quickly. I wanted to be back in the courtroom already and to hear both sides of the complaint. The young woman called out to me, "Why are you *running*? There's nothing burning!"

"Your groom's waiting for you!"

"I've waited much longer for him . . ."

Then she suddenly stopped at a little kiosk, treating me to half a glass of seltzer and a piece of candy. She handed it to me, saying, "Here, just don't end up a jerk." She was thanking me for still being a little kid and for not yet causing women any trouble.

Singer hones in on the concept of *kavanah* or intention, a major part of Hasidic religious thought, which puts greater emphasis on the thought behind the action than other Jewish streams, which focus on the action itself. Singer brings this religious perspective to secular life and suggests that intention can imbue even little actions with big meaning—as long as they are done with thought and consideration. In some ways, this connects back to the question he asked in the first article of this volume, "What's the purpose?" This spiritual question is not meant to be answered. It's meant to be asked over and over as part of an ongoing soul-searching that attaches itself, repeatedly, to our actions. Again, this all points to the development of Singer's personal brand of Jewish idealism, which he brought to bear first and foremost on his own writing. His literary practice was itself imbued, especially in the decade following the Holocaust, with an intention that brought together a faith in higher powers with a sense of purpose.

When Actions Achieve Nothing

(May 28, 1955)

One of the most important differences between the religious and the secular viewpoint consists in their approach to intention or *kavanah*—the thought itself. In religion, the thought is often more important than the action. Eating matzah on the first night of Passover isn't enough. As you fulfill this mitzvah, you have to keep the intention of the action in mind. It's not enough to recite the Shema prayer. You have to be conscious of it—and this is the case with almost everything else.

The secular viewpoint is that *kavanah*, the thought behind the action, is not important. When people give money to the poor, or to orphans, what difference does it make whether they do it because it's a mitzvah or because they want publicity? When people write good books, what does it matter if they do it for literature, money, or fame? People today presume that everyone has egotistical reasons for their actions, and they've made peace with this. If someone came and showed that Churchill or Roosevelt had done everything for the sake of their careers, or for glory, or even for money, it wouldn't make any impression on anyone. Well, so what? The main thing is that they achieved something. Even in Soviet Russia, where people are punished for saying anything against the regime—for even joking about those in power—there's no relationship to people's intentions or their personal aims. As long as they work for the party everything is fine. Careerists are both tolerated there and achieve considerable things. The truth is that communism, like capitalism, is completely based on careers and glory. The idealists who wanted to redeem humanity were shot long ago or else sent away to rot in prison.

Since people today don't take intention into account, they're forced to tolerate a great deal of lies. They're not bothered when a member of the clergy is a nonbeliever at heart or when a Reform rabbi breaks the Ten Commandments at home. They don't care about the patriotism of their generals as long as they do their jobs, or the motivations of their philanthropists. Even when it comes to love, they barely take the heart—or its intentions—into account. . . .

Yes, when we don't take intention into account and don't consider personal motives, everything becomes formal. This "formalism" is the curse of a life without intention. In an era of officialdom, judges become servants of society, defenders of everything that's beautiful and pure, and they are called "your honor"—but in the evening they go out to clubs and hang out with the outcasts they'd punished severely earlier that day. The rabbi carries out the proper ceremony, but as soon as he leaves he's an unbeliever. The poet who praises love is actually a cynic. The revolutionary who wants to destroy capitalism walks around with a fat wallet. We could go on and on this way. . . .

Ancient Jews discovered a law: without intention things can rarely turn out well. This is not only true where religion is concerned but also concerning secular matters. . . . Politics pursued without intention, without a love for truth and justice, will only serve evil. The curse of world politics lies in that politicians lack pure intentions. We can list many other domains. Sooner or later, this formalism—this superficiality—exacts a price. It undermines every initiative, neutralizes every action, drags every philanthropic or helpful act through the mud. Sodom and Gomorrah were not places where people wanted to be bad from the very outset. People in these cities surely uttered many beautiful and noble phrases. They surely had many institutions for the sick, the orphaned, the widowed. The officials stole everything—ate it all up. Sodom's formalism is best expressed by the story of the beds of Sodom. Guests were always assured a bed to spend the night in Sodom, but the lack of any intention—which is the same as having bad intentions—meant that if their feet were too long, they'd just cut them off so that they'd fit into the bed.

People raised on superficiality and formalism, on actions without intention, have one cure for every ill. In our system, everything is expressed in terms of money. In Russia, it's in terms of terror. There's a lot of crime among young people in New York? The city earmarks two and a half million dollars to fight juvenile delinquency. Jews are assimilating? We need this or that much to fight assimilation. Anything can be done with money: this is the solution of American formalism. Experience shows that it doesn't help, but superficial people know only superficial means. In communist countries, they try to cure every ill with the secret police, or with summary executions. In both systems, the work is tireless, but the more that's done, the less effective it is. . . .

Is there any direct path back to actions based on intention? No, there is no straightforward path. You can't earmark a budget for such a purpose. But the formalism of our time will do so much harm, fooling itself and others for so long, that there will have to be some reaction. History shows that every Sodom must sooner or later be destroyed. It's hard to say whether our time has achieved such a high level of superficiality, such great emptiness, that it will have to burst. But it's certainly getting close. The disgusting bankruptcy of communism, the ascent of fascism, the whining that comes from superficial and formalistic democracies—this all exposes the depth of the crisis, the kind of destruction that comes with empty talk, hollow rhetoric, and actions without *kavanah*. Jews have especially begun to feel the wasteland that action without intention has brought into our lives.

As a rule, the slightest action *with kavanah* is worth more than a thousand "big" actions *without* it. Every nation, including the Jews, waits for something, hopes for a pure action—for a return to good intentions. Even people whose hearts and minds are fully engrossed in their own superficiality feel, from time to time, the banality and ineffectiveness of their actions.

Since action without intention is an illusion, people who act this way are like the thirsty who drink salt water. The more they drink, the thirstier they are. The more they do, the less happens. . . .

Written several months before his first-ever trip to Israel—for which he was preparing not only logistically but also by learning modern Hebrew words, which he featured in a series of articles published between February 4 and April 8—this article presents a consolidation of Singer's personal philosophy after a decade of post-Holocaust spiritual reappraisal. It appeared at the time that *Satan in Goray* was first published in English, an event that was widely promoted in the pages of the *Forverts* and itself represented the beginnings of his status as a celebrated Yiddish literary figure. With this mantle, he points in this piece to the challenge not only of writing fiction that will interest readers but also acting as a spiritual leader—a secular rabbi—and the significance of such a role not only for him as an author but for Yiddish literature generally. This is also the moment when he begins framing the problem of Yiddish literature as a unique example of broader modern dilemmas, suggesting that the crisis of Yiddish is emblematic of the crisis of humanity—articulating an early version of the vision that would guide the rest of his literary career.

Is There a Way Out for Yiddish Literature?

(July 10, 1955)

Books arrive. Yiddish writers write and send their work to colleagues, adding a nice dedication. These books stand on my shelf, the new ones with the not so new, staring at me reproachfully. In reality, each book deserves not a dissertation but a trial. A literary Sanhedrin should undertake research on every new book, looking through it and comparing it to others and then issuing a verdict. A book is a piece of a person's soul. But the situation is such that souls are neglected. A voluptuous woman walking down the street will turn a thousand heads. But thought, sentiment, and human creativity are considered cheap.

Who's guilty for this cheapening? First, there's more supply than demand. Each of us has—and can get—more books than we can read. No matter how good a wine may be, when there's more than we can drink, we don't drink at all. The world has accumulated such spiritual treasures that there's no longer time or strength to enjoy them. This writer often feels that his new work is just a drop in the ocean.

People no longer live in houses that are five hundred or even two hundred years old. People don't wear clothes that were sewn many years ago. But we still have works from every generation and from every country. Contemporary writers have to compete with Homer, Dante, Tolstoy, Dostoevsky. Those writers are read much more than contemporary ones.

The second reason for this cheapening is that many people who don't have a calling for writing nevertheless write and use their sharp elbows to push their work into the literary market. Critics cannot and will not insult these writers too much, each of whom is good and right in their own eyes. There are also critics in every country who literally specialize in praising bad books. Sometimes this is done out of kindness, and sometimes there are debts owed. The result is that the number of books grows to a fantastic degree, while the better writers are often overlooked and forgotten along with the weaker or worse writers.

In the English-language market, there's at least a selection based on economics. They only publish those books for which they have buyers. They publish lots of bad and depraved books because there are lots of bad and depraved readers. They also publish good books. In the Yiddish-language market, where it mainly pays *not* to publish anything, books stand outside of the laws of supply and demand. Anyone who has put a few dollars together and wants to be an author publishes a book. Whoever has the energy and inclination to send out books to all kinds of addresses does so. The whole thing increasingly takes on the character of philanthropy. This is a sad state of affairs. The true victims are the talented writers. They will no longer have a voice if they either can't or don't want to use their own money to publish their books and then look for buyers. The situation is such that better writers, who are often a bit more embarrassed or proud, can no longer speak. The conditions are more favorable for those who are themselves writers, publishers, and customers.

Is this a hopeless situation?

Some people point out that Jewish authors sold their own books for hundreds of years. So why is this so terrible now? The answer is that, though in the olden days religious books didn't have a lot of monetary value, they still had a practical value. Every Jewish studyhouse was full of religious books. Almost every Jewish household had a bookcase. The Hebrew Bible, the Talmud, the accepted interpreters and commentators, the books on ethics—they all sold well and were reprinted countless times. People also paid good money for them. New authors tried to publish their books alongside these sellable *sforim*. The trouble with Yiddish books is that there's almost no demand for the classic works either. The standard bookcase, which new authors are supposed to try and push their way into, no longer exists.

This creates a different situation altogether. So what's the way out?

Some people believe that harsher criticism, which would tear bad work apart, might create more opportunities for better writers. There was a time when this writer held such a view. But it's hard to believe that this would improve the situation for better writers today. We have previously spoken and continue to speak of publishing houses belonging to different Yiddish organizations, but there's no reason to believe that such a publisher is interested in quality. Publishers that belong to larger organizations usually serve those closest to them in ideological terms. Journal and book publishers that toe the party line are not—and probably cannot be—overly picky. Publishers with party affiliation have the movement in mind before all else. It's where they get their money—and it's where their responsibilities lie.

The biggest trouble is that neither the self-published writers nor the party-affiliated publishers can increase the number of readers or book lovers. For people who buy books either out of pity or party loyalty, the purchase is enough. People who aren't interested in reading don't read.

The tendency has recently developed to save Yiddish literature with money. Many prizes have been created. Wealthy Jews donate money to such causes. Organizations publish books with considerable losses. But this rescue effort is superficial. No prize has ever magically endowed untalented people with talent, and books sent to party members or people who belong to all of the different movements usually sit in place like rocks. Money can save people in need, it can be used to do countless good things, but money can't lift up a literature just like money can't improve someone's personality. A literature must have readers, *interested* readers—readers who have expectations for a book and who shut themselves away, unable to put it down, until it's done. A literature must also have a large reserve of young readers whose spiritual growth is connected with books, people who get their information and knowledge about life from books. It goes without saying that a literature needs *good* writers. Do we need to add that a single good writer does more for a literature than do a hundred weak or mediocre ones? A literature is not a social movement. It doesn't need big masses. It needs just a few creative people who know how to arouse interest and, even more so, how to arouse enthusiasm.

It is precisely this last item that is lacking today more than ever in our literature. Yiddish readers were once inspired by writers like Sholem Aleichem, Y. L. Peretz, David Frishman, Hillel Zeitlin, Sholem Asch, Dovid Bergelson, I. J. Singer, Zalman Shneour, and others like them. During the periods when they wrote, they ignited in readers a combination of pleasure, suspense, wonder. We still have plenty of Yiddish writers that we can read if we want. But we lack the kinds of writers that we *really* want to read, that we almost *have* to read. I believe that this circumstance is to blame for most of the misfortunes of our Yiddish literature. If we had this kind of writing, we would still have readers for it. The same people who yawn when they look at a book or frown when you try to sell them one would run looking for such literary works. Everyone wants to have their interest aroused, their enthusiasm awakened. What people won't give for a renewed interest in life! This is the reason that hundreds of thousands of Jews are now going to Israel.

Neither political parties nor literary prizes can help with this. The only people who can help are those who feel an inner spark that can burst into flames.

In our time, we have witnessed the advent of a literature without fire. In the Soviet Union, they *constructed* a literature that inspired no one, not even the staunchest of communists. It may sound strange, but there was no communism in this literature. Instead of awakening anything, it put you to sleep, though they used plenty of grandiose words. They spoke of fire, but there was no fire burning there. Hebrew literature is now suffering from a similar problem. The language is still developing. Writers invent words and expressions. They exploit all kinds of topics. But rarely is anyone *inspired*. It lacks the stuff that makes your heart beat faster and arouses a mix of pleasure and pain. Yiddish literature in America has in recent years suffered the same sickness. You get books, but you don't feel like locking yourself up with them or going somewhere out to the country to devour them. To a great degree this is true of other literatures as well. It can be said that modern writers have lost the power to excite, to inspire, to bring joy to people's souls—not thoughtless optimism but the joy of creativity.

We cannot dwell specifically on these reasons here. But one thing is clear: Writers have to be hot in their own right if they want to warm up readers. They must themselves have an excitable spirit, a joy of creativity, an attitude toward the world, toward people, things, and higher powers—with which they can infect readers. Cold and artificial writers will never stimulate anyone. Writers must have a rich inner world and must lead deeply spiritual lives to ignite the souls of others.

Such writers are completely lacking—and, even if they did exist, the circumstances would crush them. No one can reach for the heights and maintain their character while doing all of the things that we are forced to do just to be able to keep afloat on the literary surface. You can't surround yourself with mediocre people, serving them and molding yourself to their interests, and still be a spiritual leader. It's impossible. The path to Yiddish creativity—as to any true creativity—is through internal uplifting, through grappling with the higher powers, through wanting to aspire, to yearn, to lead an intense inner life. Spiritual people cannot be overly proud, but neither can they be beggars, backslappers, or promoters of all sorts of causes, even if they are heading down the right path.

Creative people—more than any others—must be individualists. They must have relationships with other people, but these have to be conducted creatively, not merely mechanically. In the end, the crisis of Yiddish literature is the crisis of every literature. Writers have become too small and are constantly being told from all sides that they have to become even smaller.

It's no minor thing to inspire readers today. Readers have generally become smarter, less naive, and in many cases quite cynical. They have also either lived through or witnessed events that no pen can portray—that no imagination can outdo. Readers today are tough nuts to crack. Some writers try to surprise them with all kinds of tricks, phrases, literary devices—but they don't work for long. The truth is that only true greatness can uplift readers. But true greatness is not easily achieved. It can be achieved, first, by people with noble souls and, second, through consistent purification, by constantly occupying oneself with spiritual matters. Even communists in Russia have realized by now that the probing and spiritual suffering found in Tolstoy and Dostoevsky are more useful to Russia than all their contemporary propagandists and emissaries.

Yiddish readers have endured and suffered more

than all other readers. They are far more refined than we think, and it's no easy task to influence them, gain their trust, and capture their eyes and ears. Yiddish literature—and Yiddish culture as a whole—needs independent writers, people who serve no one and who can use their own spark to light a fire. The colder contemporary people are the purer and hotter the sun has to be to warm them up.

Yiddish literature has only one way out: spiritual uplifting.

Acknowledgments

Professional acknowledgments usually precede personal expressions of gratitude. But the recent period has shown that our work is sustained in large part by those closest to us. And so I want to express my deep love and appreciation to Aleza, my wife, and to our girls—Kedem Sarai, Alma Zisel, and Sinai Ruth—for being the foundation upon which this book came into existence. The months during which this book was edited and translated were some of the most challenging that we as individual Jews living in Jerusalem—and as members of a worldwide Jewish collective—have experienced in several generations. Whereas the first volume of this project evoked the spirit of those Jews who came face to face with the Holocaust, this one is addressed to anyone living today who seeks spiritual strength in order, in Singer's words, to look truth in the eye.

I also want to thank some of those friends and colleagues who have made it possible to continue the work of literature during this fraught period: Amnon Ben-Ami, Barbara Ben-Ami, Sudip Bose, Bob Boyers, the late Denis Boyles, Peter Cole, Aviva Dautch, Ofer Dynes, Adiel Guggenheim, Gail Hareven, Adina Hoffman, Gilad Jacobson, Annie Kantar Ben-Hillel, Louis Katz, Jamaica Kincaid, Eli Lederhendler, Alon Levitan, Sagit Mezamer, Velina Minkoff, Frédérique de Montblanc, Jefferey Posternak, David Reid, David Roskies, Yanai

Segal, Magda Teter, Leona Toker, Jay Tolson, Rebecca Taylor, Tom Toremans, and Val Vinokur.

Finally, I am ever indebted to the team from the Isaac Bashevis Singer Literary Trust, the Susan Schulman Literary Agency, and the Yiddish Book Center that came together once again to produce this second volume: Susan Bronson, Emelie Burl, Ezra Glinter, Jeff Hayes, Aaron Lansky, Lisa Newman, Yankl Salant, Susan Schulman, and the children of the late Israel Zamir.

Isaac Bashevis Singer (1903–1991) was a Polish-born Jewish-American author of novels, short stories, memoirs, essays, and stories for children. His career spanned nearly seven decades of literary production, much of it spent translating his own work from Yiddish into English, which he undertook with various collaborators and editors. Singer published widely during his lifetime, with nearly sixty stories appearing in *The New Yorker*, and received numerous awards and prizes, including two Newbery Honor Book Awards (1968 and 1969), two National Book Awards (1970 and 1974), and the Nobel Prize for Literature (1978). Known for fiction that portrayed 19th-century Polish Jewry as well as supernatural tales that combined Jewish mysticism with demonology, Singer was a master storyteller whose sights were set squarely on the tension between human nature and the human spirit.

David Stromberg is a writer, translator, and literary scholar. His work has appeared in *Salmagundi*, *The American Scholar*, and *Woven Tale Press*, among others. In his role as editor of the Isaac Bashevis Singer Literary Trust he has published *Old Truths and New Clichés* (Princeton University Press), a collection of Singer's essays, and a new translation of the canonical story *Simple Gimpl: The Definitive Bilingual Edition* (Restless Books). Among Stromberg's recent writing is a series of speculative essays, including "A Short Inquiry into the End of the World" (*The Massachusetts Review*), "The Eternal Hope of the Wandering Jew" (*The Hedgehog Review*), and "To Kill an Intellectual" (*The Fortnightly Review*). He is based in Jerusalem.

About White Goat Press

White Goat Press, the Yiddish Book Center's imprint, is committed to bringing newly translated work to the widest readership possible. We publish work in all genres—novels, short stories, drama, poetry, memoirs, essays, reportage, children's literature, plays, and popular fiction, including romance and detective stories.